Passport's I

MO

MW00966711

ST. PETERSBURG

FROM
**THOMAS
COOK**

PASSPORT BOOKS
a division of *NTC Publishing Group*
Lincolnwood, Illinois USA

Published by Passport Books,
a division of NTC Publishing Group,
4255 W. Touhy Avenue,
Lincolnwood (Chicago), Illinois
60646–1975 U.S.A.

Written by Chris Booth

Original photography by Ken Paterson and Jon Arnold

Edited, designed and produced by AA Publishing.
© The Automobile Association 1996.
Maps © The Automobile Association 1996.

Library of Congress Catalog Card Number: 95-73293

ISBN 0-8442-4826-6

Published by Passport Books in conjunction with AA Publishing and the Thomas Cook Group Ltd.

Color separation: BTB Colour Reproduction, Whitchurch, Hampshire, England.

Printed by Edicoes ASA, Oporto, Portugal.

Contents

About this Book

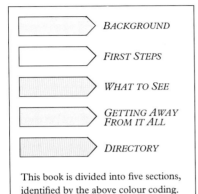

BACKGROUND

FIRST STEPS

WHAT TO SEE

GETTING AWAY
FROM IT ALL

DIRECTORY

This book is divided into five sections, identified by the above colour coding.

First Steps offers practical advice on arriving and getting around.
What to See is an alphabetical listing of places to visit, interspersed with city walks.
Getting Away From it All highlights places off the beaten track where it's possible to relax and enjoy peace and quiet.
Finally, the **Directory** provides practical information – from shopping and entertainment to children and sport, including a section on business matters. Special highly illustrated features on specific aspects of the cities appear throughout the book.

Background gives an introduction to the cities – their history, geography, politics, culture.

Products of western culture are prominent on the streets of Moscow today

BACKGROUND

'Russia is not the mind's to fathom,
The yardstick's ne'er to measure.
For hers is a stature all her own;
One can but believe in Russia.'

FYODOR TYUTCHEV
(1803–73)

Introduction

*R*ussia – few do not sense a frisson of anticipation at the mere mention of the word. The mind conjures with images of haunting natural beauty and exotic architecture, imperial extravagance and bleak communist uniformity, inspired arts, simple-hearted *joie de vivre* and chilling despotism: the land seems so familiar yet remains, at heart, a mystery.

It is a mystery which even the Russians themselves do not claim to have fathomed, but its depths and paradoxes cannot be better revealed to the foreign visitor than through the two great cities of Moscow (Moskva) and St Petersburg (Sankt Peterburg).

Both cities are at the centre of a battle to overcome the consequences of more than 70 years of communist rule. Mikhail Gorbachev's twin policies of *perestroika* and *glasnost* in the 1980s plunged the nation into the throes of reforms whose outcome is still far from guaranteed. But the new freedoms also mean Russia is open as never before to foreign tourism. The visitor to Moscow and St Petersburg is offered a unique opportunity – to be an eyewitness at the scene of the most important events in the second half of our century.

'If ever your sons should be discontented with France, try my receipt,' wrote the Marquis de Custine after a visit in the 19th century. 'Tell them to go to Russia. It is a useful journey for every foreigner: who has well examined that country will be content to live anywhere else.' The sentiment was to be echoed for another hundred years and more in travellers' tales of morose shopkeepers, police informers, inedible food and bloody-minded bureaucrats.

Though these ghosts of Russia's past have still to be fully exorcised, Moscow and St

Moscow apartment block in the 'wedding cake' style popular in the Stalinist era

A splash of oriental colour. Moscow is capital of a vast country where east and west meet

Petersburg today have so much more to recommend them. As well as the treasures of art and architecture, both cities are ablaze with an infectious, creative vitality that means a first trip to Russia will rarely be the last. To meet first hand a people who were forbidden to fraternise with westerners and of whom we in the west lived in fear for much of our lives is an unforgettable experience. And as travel becomes ever easier, the warmth and overwhelming hospitality of the Russians – less well-known but far more revealing than red flags and parades of ballistic missiles – is the impression likely to last longest. Whatever the labyrinthine mysteries of the country, it will not disappoint.

RUSSIAN FEDERATION

Geography

Situated on Russia's far western extreme, St Petersburg was once hub of a vast empire reaching 9,500km eastwards from the Baltic coast to the Pacific Ocean and almost 5,000km from the Arctic to the Caspian Sea. Today it is Moscow that, despite the collapse of the Soviet Union, remains the capital of a staggering nine time zones of Russian territory.

The basics

Built on the important Moskva river, Moscow was ideally placed to dominate trade among the Russian princedoms. It never looked back. With a population of almost 10 million, Moscow is today the world's sixth largest city and the focus of the aspirations and irritations of most of Russia's other 149 million citizens.

St Petersburg is the most northerly of the world's big cities and its five million inhabitants share the same latitude with Anchorage in Alaska. Its 44 islands straddle the delta of the Neva river on the Gulf of Finland, making for a damp and windy climate.

As both Hitler and Napoleon discovered, winter can be formidably cold, dipping as low as a record –42°C in Moscow. 'Russia has two generals in which she can trust,' Nicholas I remarked, 'Generals Janvier and Février.'

While both cities churn out machine tools, vehicles and chemicals, ever more people are turning to the once despised profession of '*biznesmyen*', trading whatever comes their way and satisfying a nation long starved of consumer goods.

The economics of reform

Economics rather than politics spelled the end for the communist system. A series of Five Year Plans had huge success in turning the USSR into an industrial giant. But growth of six per cent a year had collapsed to negative figures by the mid-1980s. Harvests rotted in the fields and life was characterised by the saying: 'We pretend to work and they pretend to pay us.'

In the end, the October Revolution proved no match for the information revolution. Herculean tractor production figures were meaningless in a world dominated by computers: in 1987, the USSR possessed just 100,000 personal computers compared with US annual production of over five million! Something had to change.

The cost of communism

Following Stalin's declaration that 'there are no fortresses that communism cannot storm', Soviet planners in quest of ever-higher economic targets wreaked havoc with the environment. A scheme to reverse the flow of Siberia's rivers was narrowly avoided, but the country is scarred by other ecological disasters.

Pollution in some industrial towns is so high that children need regular doses of pure oxygen. Lake Baikal, containing a fifth of the world's fresh water, is damaged by waste from the cellulose plants on its shores. Parts of western Russia were severely affected by radiation from the nuclear reactor fire at Chernobyl in 1986. Both Moscow and St Petersburg are periodically rocked by rumours about the emissions of their many secret factories.

Pollution combined with poor diet and hard work accounts for Russia's high child mortality rate and low life expectancy – 62 for men and 73 for women.

Mighty Russia

For all the pain of reform, Russia's natural and human wealth is unrivalled. Massive reserves of oil, coal and natural gas remain to be tapped, attracting western investors to the Siberian permafrost, while the Ural mountains comprise 2,000km of rich mineral deposits. Timber resources are similarly assured – well over half the country is densely forested. What's more, the population is highly educated; the USSR boasted nearly 15 million active scientists and engineers.

The Moskva river, viewed here from Kallininskiy Bridge, gave Moscow early trading advantage

History

988
Prince Vladimir, ruler of the Russian state in Kiev, converts to Christianity.
1147
Yuri Dolgorukiy (Long Arm) establishes Moscow at the confluence of the Moskva and Neglinnaya rivers. Moscow becomes capital of the Principality of Muscovy.
1237
Khan Batu of the Golden Horde sacks Moscow. Tartar domination is to last for two-and-a-half centuries.
1453
The fall of Constantinople. Moscow henceforth is referred to as the 'Third and Last Rome'. The Byzantine double-headed eagle becomes the emblem of state.
1584
Ivan IV ('the Terrible') dies. Brutal regimentation of a poor land and people has brought Muscovy from an occupied city state to a great European power.
1613
Mikhail Romanov is elected Tsar of all the Russias; his dynasty will last till 1917.
1682
Peter the Great's accession to the throne aged 10.
1703
Peter founds St Petersburg on 16 May.
1712
Moscow razed by fire. St Petersburg is proclaimed the new capital.

1789
The French Revolution quashes Catherine the Great's experiment with liberalism.
1812
Napoleon invades Russia. Muscovites burn their city to drive out the invaders.
1825
Decembrists' revolt, led by educated officers later banished to Siberia or executed.
1854
The Crimean War lays bare the backwardness of Russian society.
1861
Alexander II's decree abolishing serfdom.
1894
Nicholas II ascends the throne.
1905
Attempted revolution in both Moscow and St Petersburg results in the introduction of a constitution and an elected assembly.
1917
The February revolution leads to the abdication of Nicholas II. A provisional government is in power till the Bolshevik *putsch* on 25 October. On 16 November Moscow is restored as capital.
1918
The tsar and family are executed. Civil war and foreign intervention last till 1921.

Moscow's founder Yuri Dolgorukiy

1922
The Union of Soviet Socialist Republics is founded.
1924
Lenin's death on 24 January followed by power struggle (from which Stalin emerges victorious). St Petersburg – renamed Petrograd in 1914 – becomes Leningrad.
1928
The first Five Year Plan collectivises farms, leading to famine and the death of an estimated 5 million.
1934
The assassination of Kirov, Leningrad's Party chief, heralds a period of great purges and show trials.
1941
The Soviets enter World War II. Leningrad is under siege and German troops reach the outskirts of Moscow. Some 20 million die during the war.
1953
Death of Stalin.
1956
Khrushchev's 'Secret Speech' to the 20th Party Congress denounces Stalin and initiates a limited and brief thaw.
1962
The Cuban Missile Crisis brings the world to the brink of nuclear war.
1964
Krushchev is replaced as General Secretary of the Soviet Communist Party by Leonid Brezhnev.
1979
The USSR invades Afghanistan.
1980
The Moscow Olympics are boycotted by the USA.
1985
Mikhail Gorbachev becomes Communist Party General Secretary in March and introduces *glasnost* (openness) and *perestroika* (restructuring).

1986
Human rights campaigner Andrei Sakharov is released from internal exile.
1987
Boris Yeltsin is sacked as Moscow Party boss after openly attacking Gorbachev.
1989
First democratic elections take place. Revolutions throughout the Soviet bloc lead to the fall of the Berlin Wall.
1990
Yeltsin tears up his Party card in front of millions of TV viewers.
1991
The citizens of Leningrad vote to restore the city's name to St Petersburg in June. The attempted communist coup on 19 August dissolves in incompetence two days later. Yeltsin declares the Communist Party illegal. The USSR is dissolved, and the Commonwealth of Independent States (CIS) is formed in December. Gorbachev resigns on Christmas Day.
1992
'Shock therapy' introduced, abolishing price controls overnight on 2 January. Reform is deadlocked by parliament.
1993
Yeltsin dissolves parliament on 21 September. Violent demonstrations by communists and nationalists in Moscow free the besieged parliament on 3 October. Yeltsin crushes the uprising with tank bombardment the following day – 138 are killed. Reformists are trounced in the December elections, the new parliament is controlled by communists and Vladimir Zhirinovsky's ultra-nationalist Liberal Democratic Party. A new constitution is adopted.
1994
Yeltsin orders troops into the breakaway republic of Chechnya, suffering heavy losses militarily and in the opinion polls.

OCTOBER 1917

Glorified in countless films, novels and paintings, the 'Great October Revolution' was more akin to a vaudeville farce than the dawn of the regime that was to grip Russia for over 70 years.

Vladimir Ulyanov 'Lenin' (1870–1924), in hiding and disguised by a badly-fitting wig and glasses, desperately harangued his colleagues to start a revolution which most of them, including Stalin, were against. Despite their name, meaning 'The Majority', Lenin's Bolsheviks were few and only one of many opposition factions. Knowing that they had no hope of winning elections scheduled for November, Lenin was determined to grab power by force, and on the night of 25 October (7 November in the 'New Style' – Western – calendar), the Bolsheviks sent troops to occupy key positions in Petrograd. Not a shot was fired.

Lenin penned a notice declaring the government deposed which was pasted around the city the next morning. Petrograd was unmoved: according to eyewitness accounts, offices and shops opened on time and opera-lovers looked forward to Chaliapin's evening performance at the Mariinskiy Theatre.

A haphazard siege of the Winter Palace, where the government unconcernedly sat on, was organised. Lenin emerged from hiding to make a

Scenes of the Revolution: fact or fancy?

revolutionaries had to make do with a blank shell.

Far from the frontal assault of grizzled workers, popularised in Sergei Eisenstein's film *Days of October*, the first Bolshevik forces slipped into the building through open windows. The final death toll – five – resulted from stray bullets rather than spirited resistance by the Provisional Government, which was finally arrested and led away a little after 2am the morning after.

short appearance at the Petrograd Soviet, the assembly of opposition parties, informing it that the worldwide socialist revolution had begun that night.

The 'storm' began at 9.40pm when a shot from the cruiser *Aurora*, moored downstream, broke the peace. But since the ship had just completed a refit, there were no live rounds and the

Politics

Steeped in ethnic conflict and economic chaos, the mighty Soviet Union lurched to an undignified halt on Christmas Day 1991, when Mikhail Gorbachev resigned the presidency of an extinct superpower. Over half a century of communist rule was over.

The *Ancien Régime*

Article 6 of the Soviet Union enshrined the role of the Communist Party and its 20 million members as 'the leading and guiding force of Soviet society'. Every farm and factory had its Party cell which supervised decisions emanating from the Politburo. The nerve centre of the system, the Politburo met every Thursday under the guidance of the Party General Secretary, the country's leader.

The Party appointed all key officials, and its élite were rewarded with special medical care, access to closed shops and imported goods, country houses and hunting reserves. They were, in the subtle Russian distinction, *lyudi* rather than *naseleniye* – 'people' rather than 'population'. Their children could look forward to easy entry into the Party, university and the choicest jobs. The system, it seemed, was self-perpetuating.

The carrot …

Under Brezhnev, the Soviet Union grew fat and lazy in the period known as *zastoi* (stagnation). Housing was cheap – a few roubles a month – with heating, phones and water thrown in. Employment was guaranteed by the constitution, hence attendance at the work place was not considered crucial. Bribery was rife and pilfering from the factory was thought the norm. Holidays on the Black Sea coast were within reach of many; the rest received subsidised vacations at factory-owned sanatoria.

Brezhnev rewarded himself with a chestful of medals, five country estates and a collection of foreign luxury cars.

The grim collective face of Soviet leadership taking the salute in Red Square

December 1988: Mikhail Gorbachev meets Ronald Reagan and George Bush in New York

... and the stick

Life was so obviously good that Khrushchev declared opposition to communism a disease of the mind: 'Clearly the mental state of such people is not normal.' High-profile dissidents might be asked to leave the country; others were locked in secret hospitals for psychiatric treatment; the remainder were consigned to labour camps in Siberia or within the Arctic Circle.

The KGB, the acronym for the 'State Security Committee', had a staff of 700,000 and as many informers. Although its powers were cut after Stalin's purges, when it arrested an estimated 8 million, it was still all pervading, amassing files and acting on the prompting of the *donos*, the system of secret denunciation of workers by their colleagues.

The KGB grew again when Andropov, its former chief, became Party General Secretary. International phone lines introduced for the 1980 Olympics were cut, printed material required a permit to be sent abroad, and fines were introduced for citizens thought to have excessively helped foreign visitors.

A walk on the beach

'We can't go on like this,' Gorbachev confided in December 1984 to his old friend Eduard Shevardnadze as they strolled on the beach at Pitsunda in the Caucasus. Something had to be done, they agreed, to revitalise a stagnant economy less capable than ever of meeting the demands of modern life and facing a hostile adversary in Ronald Reagan's Pentagon.

The tractor driver's son from the south of Russia was to get his chance three months later, elected General Secretary of the Politburo on the death of Chernenko in March 1985.

ТРУДОВАЯ СТОЛИЦА

Perestroika and Glasnost

Gorbachev's early efforts to jump-start the country were a flop – the campaign for *uskorenie* (acceleration) was treated with scepticism by a weary nation, while an anti-alcohol drive alienated workers by depriving them of the one form of escapism that didn't require an exit visa.

Realising that root and branch reforms were unavoidable if the Party was to survive, Gorbachev coined the term *perestroika* – 'reconstruction' – and set about decentralising the economy.

A key role in this was to be played by *glasnost*, or 'openness', by which ordinary people would have their say and hence galvanise complacent bureaucrats and corrupt directors into action. At the same time, Gorbachev strove to halt the arms race and occupation of Afghanistan which were pointlessly bankrupting the domestic economy.

The beginning of the end

Lionised abroad for tolerating the destruction of the Berlin Wall in 1989, Gorbachev's popularity at home fell as his reforms ran into the sand. G*lasnost* assumed a momentum of its own, breaking the Party's monopoly of political power, sparking industrial unrest and unleashing ethnic tensions.

Instead of using it to resuscitate communism as Gorbachev had hoped, the people took *glasnost* at face value and pressed for ever wider freedoms. At the 1990 May Day parade in Red Square, Gorbachev was booed from the podium on Lenin's mausoleum.

Gorbachev met his nemesis in the president of the Russian Republic, Boris Yeltsin, who had already torn up his Party membership card in public. Yeltsin was democratically elected and he used his mandate to declare Russian independence in June 1991, forcing Gorbachev to agree to the drafting of a new Union Treaty.

The August *putsch*

For exasperated communists, this was the final straw. On 19 August, the State Committee for the State of Emergency announced that Gorbachev was ill and that they were assuming power. Crowds flocked to defend the White House, the Russian government building, where they were addressed by Yeltsin standing on top of a tank. Support for the coup failed to materialise and the conspirators surrendered after two days.

Yeltsin suspended the Communist Party, and the remaining republics declared independence, leaving Gorbachev powerless till the year's end.

His policies of *perestroika* and *glasnost* had proved incapable of shaking the USSR out of its Brezhnevian torpor. Instead, they hastened the collapse of the communist system and presided over the end of the Cold War.

The New Order

Perestroika and Boris Yeltsin's struggle for political reform created for the first time the structure of a democratic state. Under the 1993 Constitution, a powerful President is checked by the State Duma (parliament), whose members are elected by universal suffrage. Fair play is ensured by the Constitutional Court. Political parties range from the 'democrats', like Russia's Choice, to the 'red-brown' opposition of the reformed Communist Party and the extreme nationalist Liberal Democrats. In between are Women of Russia, the Christian Democrats, the Beer Lovers' Party and many more.

In practice, parliament is incapacitated by fractious quarrels, while the president ignores it, preferring to legislate by decree. Unelected advisory groups in the Kremlin are more influential than official government bodies. And all the really big politics goes on behind the closed doors of the shadowy Security Council, uniting the president, the defence and interior ministers and the chairman of the KGB's successor, the Federal Counterintelligence Committee.

Russians seem only mildly interested at best. Now the flush of democratic enthusiasm has subsided, local elections are regularly voided by insufficient turn-out. The government is regarded as a self-serving élite and the parliament as an irrelevant circus. Few understand the need for a constitution which is systematically broken and a growing number 'yearn for a strong hand' to whip the country into order.

Boris Yeltsin (inset) rose to power after 1991's failed coup

Culture

*R*ussians are fiercely proud of their deep cultural heritage, both in the arts and in daily life. Here peasant *joie de vivre* meets abstract philosophy, in a culture that has been moulded by centuries of foreign invasion, despotic government and Orthodox piety. There is no better introduction to it than a stay in Moscow or St Petersburg.

The arts

A love of the arts is by no means an élite diversion in Russia, where concerts and exhibitions are heavily subsidised and the national poet, Alexander Pushkin (1799–1837), is cherished with a passion far exceeding that of the English for Shakespeare or the Germans for Goethe.

Many artists enjoy a kind of cult status generally reserved in the west for pop stars. The reason is simple: under autocratic rule, producing subversive work carried the risk of imprisonment or exile if the tsar was displeased. Likewise, after 1917, artists denied membership of the official state union were liable to imprisonment as 'social parasites'. Their work would be secretly shared with trusted friends late in the evening around the kitchen table.

Russkaya Dusha

The 'Russian soul' – *russkaya dusha* – is more legend than fact, some say. At a time when burgers and BMWs are more in demand than balalaikas, the fabled Russian character can seem no deeper than the lacquer on the cheap nesting dolls sold at tourist flea markets.

But as many foreigners will agree, there is a certain quality to chance acquaintances in Moscow and St Petersburg that remains uniquely Russian. The quality is one of contradiction – a cross between public conformity and private dreams of anarchy, ruthless realism combined with sugary sentimentalism, striking rudeness on the street contrasted with overwhelming generosity to guests. Russians complain about the price of cabbages and wax lyrical about frost on the hawthorn in the same breath.

The *Mir*

One explanation is that most city-dwellers are only a generation or two removed from the countryside and its traditions of rigid

Chess *al fresco* is a popular Russian pastime

collectivism. Outsiders are treated with suspicion, insiders are doted on and nonconformists are shunned: the Russian word for 'peasant community' is the same as that for the 'world' – *mir*.

Sometimes the result is plain bigotry. A streak of anti-Semitism runs deep in the national tradition, and even today a vocal element in every political demonstration blames everything from the October Revolution to the price of Coca-Cola on 'Zionist conspirators'.

Belief and superstition

Despite decades of state-sponsored atheism, Russians are, in the widest sense, a strikingly religious people. The Orthodox church is in full flourish again, as the shining new belltowers above the cities' rooftops testify. On a different level, from the adoration of Lenin to the post-Soviet fascination with television hypnotists and cure-all medicines, Russians have an unquenchable thirst for the improbable.

Westernisers and Slavophiles

Neither truly a part of Europe nor of Asia, Russia's fate has for centuries been hotly disputed between those who want to modernise the country on western

lines and those who believe in a distinct, Slavic way forward. The two camps have agreed on only one thing – that an answer must be found to the eternal question: '*shto dyela*t'? ('What is to be done?'). Those *zapadniki* ('westernisers'), such as Peter the Great, who tried to turn Russia towards Europe, often did so with

'Matryoshka' doll and balalaika group: aspects of traditional Russia

Asian barbarity. Meanwhile, the *slavyanofili* ('Slavophiles') declared Orthodox Russia's messianic role in the world but had no practical plan of action beyond extolling the peasant as a model of social organisation.

The debate is passionately pursued today as democrats battle for World Bank loans and European Union membership while nationalists and communists cry for a yet-to-be-defined Russian way.

Haves and Have Nots

*T*he Soviet Union was never the land of equality preached by socialist propaganda, despite the firm promises of Nikita Khrushchev that communism would be perfected by 1980. But when the system finally disintegrated, the population was plunged into a confusing economic free-for-all which has left one part cruising the streets in imported Lincolns and Mercedes and the other, much larger part struggling desperately to make ends meet.

instantly and a bankrupt state could do nothing to support the losers: the minimum monthly pension in late 1994 stood at not much more than 30,000 roubles, or less than 10 US dollars at the going rate.

The Moscow and St Petersburg metro systems are thronged with people selling bread, vodka, lottery tickets and ball-point pens late into the night. Qualified scientists, teachers and doctors often resort to selling souvenirs at tourist markets or importing cheap Chinese clothing to sell at home.

But the winners have become very rich, very quickly. Whether communist-era bureaucrats who have retained their posts in the new society or mafia-like racketeers, they have exploited the chaos of the transition to market economics, making huge sums exporting oil and raw materials or taking a hefty percentage of business and restaurant turnovers. Russia's new breed of *biznismyen* has lost little time in carving up the 'Wild East'.

When artificially-controlled prices were freed in 1992, inflation spiralled out of control, eliminating savings almost overnight. One US dollar bought 90 roubles then; three years later, it bought almost 4,500. A two-tier society was formed

Contrasting aspects of Moscow shopping

СТАНЦИЯ НАЗНАЧЕНИЯ		ВРЕМЯ В ПУТИ
● АДЛЕР		52·00
● АЛМА-АТА		90·05
⊕ АРХАНГЕЛЬСК		28·35
⊕ АСТРАХАНЬ		45·21
⊕ БАБАЕВО		8·
⊕ БОРОВИЧИ		
● БРЯНСК		
● ВЕСЬЕГОНСК		14
⊕ ВОЛГОГРАД		38·5
⊕ ВОЛОГДА		14·01
⊕ ВОРОНЕЖ		24·36
⊕ ГОРЬКИЙ		18·12
⊕ ЕВПАТОРИЯ		19·19
⊕ ИЖЕВСК		36·40
● ИВАНОВО		17·33
⊕ КАЗАНЬ		28·12
⊕ КАЛУГА		20·00
⊖ КИСЛОВОДСК		49·54
⊕ КОТЛАС		26·15
⊕ КУРСК		20·41
⊕ МАРИУПОЛЬ		38·08
⊕ МИН. ВОДЫ		
● МОСКВА		9·32
● МОСКВА		18·19
● МОСКВА		6·20
● МОСКВА		4·59
● МОСКВА		9·04
● МОСКВА		6·03
● МОСКВА		8·45
● МОСКВА		8·23
● МОСКВА		8·00
● МОСКВА		8·25
● МОСКВА		8·05
● МОСКВА		8·10
● МОСКВА		9·14
● МОСКВА		8·30
● МОСКВА		8·31
⊕ МУРМАНСК		37·42
● МУРМАНСК		48·37
⊕ МУРМАНСК		29·54
● МУРМАНСК		29·13
⊕ НЕВЕЛЬ		15·08
⊕ НИЖНИЙ ТАГИЛ		46·09
● НОВГОРОД		2·40
● НОВГОРОД		4·10
● НОВОРОССИЙСК		47·16
● ОМСК		58·14
● ПЕСТОВО		11·27
⊕ ПЕТРОЗА		9·18
⊕ ПИКА		5·44
⊕ РЖЕВ		10·00
⊕ САМА		48·20
⊕ СВЕРДЛ		
⊕ СВЕРДЛ		
⊕ СВЕ		

FIRST STEPS

'Russia is a riddle wrapped in a
mystery inside an enigma.'
WINSTON CHURCHILL

First Steps

*I*t takes a little courage to choose Russia as a holiday destination. The country is still ill equipped to deal with modern tourism, to say nothing of the constant political ferment, strange alphabet and abundant travellers' tales of stonewalling bureaucrats and surly restaurant staff. But a thoroughly rewarding trip is well within the grasp of any visitor armed with a sense of humour and a few basic ground rules.

The pace of change

Russia is in a state of total upheaval in the wake of the collapse of communism and this naturally makes itself felt for the foreign visitor too. Those expecting to dine out for a handful of roubles or take a taxi from Moscow to Vladivostok for a packet of cigarettes will find that times have changed unimaginably rapidly.

Moscow and St Petersburg can no longer be thought of as cheap destinations. Neither are westerners the richest people on the streets. The introduction of the free market has created a two-class society of the super-rich and the super-poor. Middle-range services have folded because ordinary people cannot afford them and the new rich prefer classier, luxury establishments. The result is that both cities are short on easily affordable hotels and restaurants and that most shops stock either low-quality domestic goods or top-of-the-range imported luxuries. Moscow was recently ranked the fourth most expensive city in the world! Similarly, the once ridiculously low cost of admission tickets to sights has been eliminated by the widespread introduction of surcharges for foreigners.

Some things are still remarkably cheap, though. Trains, public transport, theatre and concert tickets are the best value.

When to come

There can be nothing more Russian than the crisp frosts of winter, ice on the Neva and snow falling upon the golden cupolas of Moscow's churches. Likewise, there can be nothing more unpleasant than permanently frozen fingers and wet feet. To avoid too much of the latter, the

Trolleybuses on Nevskiy
Prospekt, St Petersburg

Moscow's busy Leningrad railway station, the terminal for trains to St Petersburg

best time for a winter trip is late November through to early January before the really heavy frosts or the slush of the March thaw.

In the warmer season, August and July can be suffocating in both Moscow and St Petersburg. The air is fresher around May and September and if the weather holds, these are perhaps the most attractive times of the year. To catch the legendary St Petersburg White Nights, when the sun virtually never sets and the whole city celebrates, plan your trip for the end of June or beginning of July.

Visas and arrival
All foreign nationals require a visa to enter Russia which will only be issued on a full passport. Bear in mind when planning your trip that the process of issuing a visa can be extremely lengthy and subject to unpredictable delays. Make sure you leave yourself sufficient

time before departure to cover all eventualities – as much as a month. (For more information on the various visas on offer, see page 178.)

Arrival at the airport can go smoothly but it is best to prepare for lengthy queues at passport control and customs. Although there is a green channel at the customs barrier, hard currency is considered declarable and if you have more than $50 or the equivalent you must join the queue at the red channel anyway. You will have to fill in a currency declaration form which *must* be retained until departure. (See page 180 for customs procedures in detail.)

Members of tour groups or guests of western-style hotels will probably be met at the airport. Everyone else must negotiate a taxi ride to their destination with the dozens of private cab drivers waiting in the arrivals hall. (See **Arriving**, page 178, for more information.)

Coping with the language

Nothing will increase the pleasure and ease of your trip to Russia more than a few hours at home spent mastering the Cyrillic alphabet. Although the task seems daunting, the value later is immeasurable for working out metro stations and street names (few signs are bilingual in St Petersburg; none are in Moscow). You will also be able to pronounce words and destinations – Russian is basically a phonetic language and most words are spoken just as they are spelled.

A handful of polite words learnt at home will go a long way towards melting the icy glare of even the most unhelpful official.

(See pages 183–4 for an introduction to basic words and phrases.)

Organising your time

Moscow and St Petersburg offer an astounding range of sights and activities for even the most demanding visitor. You will only be able to cover a fraction of them in the course of a normal trip, so it's worth sorting out priorities in advance. Most of the major sights in both cities are conveniently grouped near the centre; some, such as the Kremlin or the Hermitage, require most of a day to do them justice. Minor points of interest, such as less well-known museums and churches, are often spread far apart and the travelling involved is easy to underestimate. Don't feel obliged to trudge from one landmark to another – remember to save some enthusiasm for that trip to the ballet, five-course meal or ice-hockey game in the evening!

Orientation

Moscow is planned like a cartwheel with major arteries branching out from the

Kremlin (Kreml) and linked by a series of concentric ring roads. The first is the Bulvar (Boulevard Ring), which starts and stops at (but does not cross) the Moscow river, on either side of the Kremlin. The next ring road is the

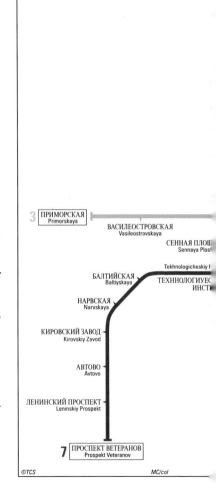

Sadovaya (Garden Ring), a heaving multi-lane highway encircling the city centre. (Note: it does *not* coincide with the circle line of the metro.)

Finally, the Outer Ring Road (MKAD – Moskovskoye Koltsevaya Avtodoroga) defines the city's limits far on the outskirts of town.

St Petersburg is simpler, with most points of interest grouped on, around or at the ends of Nevskiy Prospekt, the city's backbone.

ST PETERSBURG METRO

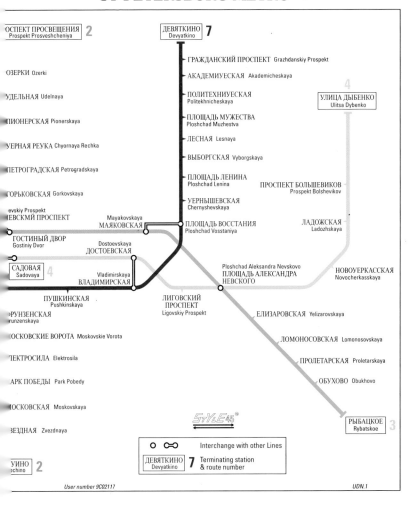

Driving

Driving around Moscow and St Petersburg is technically possible but not recommended.

Little has changed since the last century when the writer Nikolai Gogol observed: 'What Russian does not love fast driving? How could his soul, which is so eager to whirl round and round, to forget everything in a mad carousel, to exclaim sometimes: To hell with it all! ... How could his soul not love it?'

Russians overtake on both sides, aim for gaps in the traffic which don't exist and mercilessly refuse to give way to timid foreign drivers. In addition, the roads are riddled with potholes and governed by an extremely arcane highway code.

For the undaunted, there are plenty of car rental agencies in both cities.

(See page 181 for more information.)

The unpredictable

Economic and political turmoil has only added to the ever-present element of unpredictability in Russian life. Prepare to find museums unexpectedly closed – for political reasons or for conversion into a nightclub. Don't be surprised if a favourite restaurant slides dramatically down- or up-market in the course of a week; nor if the exchange rate does the same. Anticipate that booking offices may be closed, as the sign will say, 'for technical reasons'. Be prepared to be denied access to an apparently public bar for not knowing the right people. It's all part of the adventure.

Public transport

As in any city, getting the hang of the public transport system in Moscow and St Petersburg takes practice. While you can conceivably do without using it, a

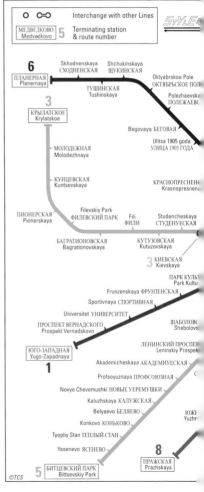

few tactical stops on the metro (underground) network will dramatically save time and energy between sights. Buses, trams and trolleybuses are trickier to master, but where essential, they are mentioned in the text. To begin with, try

trolleybuses nos 10 and B for negotiating Moscow's Garden Ring, while in St Petersburg, nos 1 and 7 cut out the footwork on Nevskiy Prospekt. (See pages 186–7 for detailed information on travelling by public transport.)

MOSCOW METRO

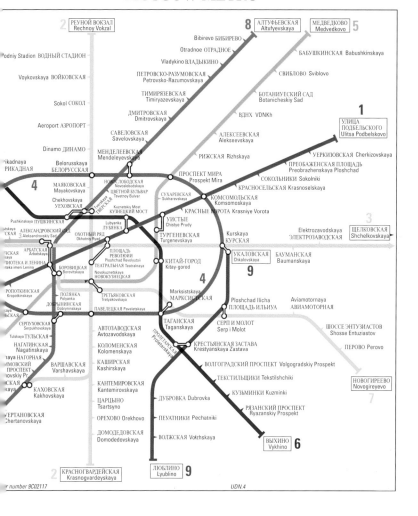

Sight-seeing survival

Here are a few tips for the determined sightseer in Russia.

• Check opening times very carefully: not only do they vary wildly from one place to another, but most places of interest are closed for an extra day near the end of the month for cleaning. Some places, like the Kremlin, even have different times for each of the attractions within.

• Bring refreshments of your own and any toiletries you may require; few sights have a fraction of the conveniences western tourists are accustomed to.

• You must remove your coat and deposit bags at the cloakroom. You will also be expected to don felt overshoes in museums and galleries.

• And if you wish to avoid an embarrassing scene with the fierce old ladies who guard every museum and monument across the land, don't touch anything!

THOMAS COOK'S RUSSIA

Thomas Cook organised his first 'Grand Tour' of Imperial Russia in 1887, promising his patrons 'an acquaintance with peoples of many nations' and 'the services of a competent personal Conductor' all for the princely sum of 137 pounds sterling, first-class steamer fares included.

Later, a contributor to Cook's Traveller's Gazette *in 1930 marvelled how 'in buildings which until a few short years ago were palaces of the Tsars, the affairs of the most modern state in the world are settled…'*

Yeliseev's, Moscow's gourmet food store on Tverskaya Ulitsa: luxury if you can afford it

WHAT TO SEE

'[Moscow] is neither Europe nor Asia:
it is Russia – and it is Russia's heart.'

MARQUIS DE CUISINE
(1790–1857)
The Empire of the Tsar

'We are fated here by nature
To cut through a window onto Europe.'

ALEXANDER PUSHKIN
(1799–1837)
Peter the Great founding St Petersburg in
The Bronze Horseman

Moskva
(Moscow)

'*M*oscow! How much is combined in this sound for the Russian heart!' wrote the national poet Alexander Pushkin in the 19th century. The city is the cultural focus of Russia, enshrining civic ceremony and the Orthodox faith, great musical traditions and theatrical excellence. Most of all, it is the incarnation of that subtle blend of anarchy and nostalgia which the nation proudly refers to as the 'Russian Soul'.

A fight for survival

Since its humble inception in 1147 as a small encampment overlooking the Moskva river, Moscow has suffered frequent attack. First came the Mongols – or Tartars – who sacked the city, gathered slaves and collected tribute from the residents. Fear of the 'Tartar yoke' lasted until the 16th century – they last levelled the city in 1571. Next came the Poles, who occupied the city for two years at the beginning of the following century.

Red Square: the spiritual heart of Moscow

Relative peace ensued as St Petersburg assumed the mantle of imperial capital until, in 1812, Napoleon entered the Kremlin. A desperate population resorted to setting the city ablaze to drive him out. Finally, in 1941, Hitler boasted: 'In a few weeks, we shall be in Moscow. I will raze that damned city and in its place construct an artificial lake with central lighting.' He failed.

The old and the new

As capital of the Soviet Union, Moscow grew rapidly from a picturesque,

MOSCOW TOWN PLAN

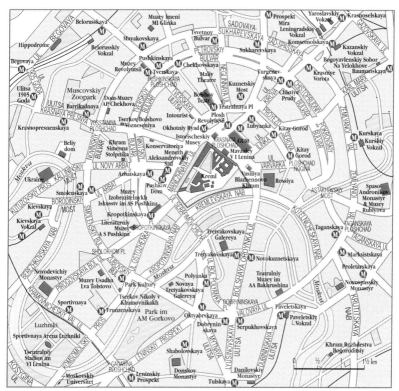

medieval city into a sprawling, modern metropolis. Soviet planners blasted away old quarters of the city to erect massive hotels and force through multi-lane highways. Stalin ordered the construction of the vast gothic skyscrapers which today dominate the skyline.

But Moscow retains plenty of its old character and remains a Russian, rather than Soviet city. Whole streets are lined with the neo-classical mansions of the old aristocracy. Wandering into a back alley off the main roads can be like entering a time-warp as you stumble across delicate

Orthodox churches and courtyards little changed from the time of Tolstoy and Dostoevsky.

The Muscovites

Russia is a land of over 100 separate nationalities, from Tuvans to Kalmyks and Chukchi to Circassians, as well as the Russians themselves. A true Muscovite is a rare individual indeed. But whatever their origin, the 10 million or so inhabitants of Moscow are proud of their city, for all its eccentricities and hardships.

ALEKSANDROVSKIY SAD (Alexander Gardens)

Tucked under the Kremlin's western wall, the Alexander Gardens are best known for the solemn Tomb of the Unknown Soldier. The gardens were laid out for Tsar Alexander I in 1821 over the bricked-in Neglinnaya river – which might account for the characteristic coolness they afford in summer after a hot afternoon's visit to the Kremlin. *Manezhnaya Ulitsa. Free. Metro: Aleksandrovskiy Sad, Biblioteka imeni Lenina.*

Detail from the Tomb of the Unknown Soldier

Borovitskaya Ploshchad (Borovitskaya Square)

Adjoining the southern end of the gardens, this busy intersection is dominated by the striking Pashkov Dom (Pashkov House), built between 1784 and 1786. It now shares some of the 29 million volumes of the neighbouring Biblioteka imeni Lenina (Lenin Library), Europe's largest library.

Manezhnaya Ploshchad (Manège Square)

The low, columned building alongside the upper half of the gardens is the former imperial riding school, or Manège. Stalin used it as a garage for the Kremlin's automobile fleet and nowadays it serves as an exhibition hall.

Memorial Mogila Neizvestnogo Soldata (The Tomb of the Unknown Soldier)

The memory of World War II is deeply felt in Russia. Estimated at 20 million, the number of Soviet deaths will never be precisely known. Official delegations and newlyweds lay wreaths here on the grave of an infantry man killed at the 41km point on Leningradskoye Shosse (Leningrad Highway), the closest German soldiers came to Moscow. The inscription beneath the eternal flame reads: 'Your name is unknown, your deeds immortal.'

Obelisk

Under Lenin's orders, the first of countless memorials to the Revolution was unveiled in the Alexander Gardens in 1918. It was previously a monument celebrating the tercentenary of the Romanov dynasty, but the Bolsheviks knocked off the double-headed eagle and inscribed the names of socialist thinkers.

THE LAST OF THE COMMUNISTS

The statue of Karl Marx opposite the Bolshoy Theatre and the former Lenin Museum on Ploshchad Revolyutsii are favourite gathering points of diehard communists (*metro: Ploshchad Revolyutsii*). Mostly pensioners, the true believers are now more of a tourist sight than a real political force. Demonstrations take place most Sundays, but the really big crowds gather on 7 November, Revolution Day, and May Day.

The White House, home of the Russian Parliament

BELIY DOM
(White House)

Gleaming on the banks of the river opposite the Stalinist skyscraper Ukraine Hotel, the White House stands at the heart of the battle for Russia's political future. As the House of Soviets of the Russian Federation, it was the site of makeshift barricades against the abortive 1991 coup, when crowds swamped half-hearted tank commanders sent in to restore order.

In October 1993, this time as the Russian Parliament, the building was the focus of hostilities between President Yeltsin and hardline deputies. It looked, briefly, as though the communists were triumphant until Yeltsin ordered tanks to bombard the building into submission: 138 were killed. Repairs cost over $80 million.

Graffiti, pockmarked walls and crucifixes to the fallen mark the battle zone today on the back streets behind what is now a heavily fenced-off House of the Russian Government. *Konyushkovskaya Ulitsa. Metro: Krasnopresnenskaya.*

ZHIRINOVSKY'S PARTY

Loved and loathed in equal measure across the country, Vladimir Zhirinovsky and his inappropriately named Liberal Democratic Party rely on a mixture of nationalism, anti-Semitism and plain outrage to fuel their notoriety. He calls for the Russian occupation of Alaska and threatened to erect giant fans on the borders of the Baltics to blow radiation on them if they resisted plans for a new USSR. His headquarters on Rybnikov Pereulok (*metro: Turgenevskaya*) include a kiosk called Zhirinovsky's Rock Shop selling T-shirts and his own brand of vodka.

ARISTOCRATIC RUSSIA

Neglected and flaking, long converted into clinics, libraries and warehouses or more recently bought up by banks and casinos, the dozens of neo-classical mansions on the boulevards of Moscow and back streets of St Petersburg were once thriving enclaves of Russian aristocratic life.

The country was awash with nobility: nearly two million individuals could claim aristocratic lineage on the eve of the Revolution. While many were gentry in name only, masters of tiny estates in the provinces, others such as Moscow's Golitsyns and the Yusupovs of St Petersburg were fantastically rich, their wealth measured in the number of serfs, or 'souls', they possessed.

Theirs was a far cry from the Russia of ordinary people. Few conversed in Russian, for French was considered the language of a gentleman. Education for ambitious young men was experienced abroad or under the supervision of foreign tutors, while the life of young women revolved about the St Petersburg season. Winters were spent on the Mediterranean coast and politics were largely left to lesser mortals.

Even minor nobles had as house servants a baker, pastrycook, mead-maker, brewer, locksmith, carpenter, saddler and tin-plater, in addition to chefs, coachmen, butlers and washerwomen. Prince Kropotkin, a prominent anarchist in later life, remembers in his childhood 'a dozen

men to wait upon us at dinner time (one man, plate in hand, standing behind each person seated at the table), and girls innumerable in the maidservants' room – how could anyone do with less than this?'.

But for many it was a stultifying existence. One of Russia's great novels, Ivan Goncharov's *Oblomov*, is devoted

Le Petit Journal

SUPPLÉMENT ILLUSTRÉ

Huit pages : CINQ centimes

SAMEDI 11 MARS 1893

Turn-of-the-century pictures of upper-class life. Above: *The Restaurant* (Russian School). Left: the tsar attending a ball at the French embassy

to the syndrome of 'the superfluous man' that beset a class divorced from its nation and powerless to prevent its own demise. The poet Alexander Pushkin lamented in a letter to a friend: 'I am condemned to live among these orangutans at the most interesting moment of our century!'

Churches and Cathedrals

*T*ravellers in the 19th century never ceased to be amazed at the sight of Moscow's myriad golden cupolas – said by tradition to number '40 times 40' – and the incomparable sound from her belfries as the call to prayer rang across the city. Hundreds of churches were demolished or ransacked under the Soviets; today the Orthodox religion is in the throes of a powerful surge in popularity (see pages 52–3), and many of the capital's finest holy buildings are already restored to their pre-Revolutionary splendour.

The most interesting churches and cathedrals not covered elsewhere in the text are listed below.

The elegant façade of Yelokhovskiy Cathedral

BOGOYAVLENSKIY SOBOR NA YELOKHOVE (Yelokhovskiy Cathedral)
By legend the birthplace of the holy fool St Basil, the cathedral (1845) is among Moscow's most revered, serving as the Patriarch's headquarters following his ejection by the communists from the Kremlin. The atmosphere of the resplendent interior during an evening service is unforgettable. *Ulitsa Yelokhovskaya (Spartakovskaya) 15. Tel: 267 7591. Metro: Baumanskaya.*

KHRAM POKROVA NA FILYAKH (Church of the Intercession at Fili)
Although for long not a working church, this is well worth a visit as one of the most striking examples of Muscovite high baroque architecture. Icons from the Rublyov Museum of

Interior decoration in the colourful Church of St Nicholas of the Weavers

All-Russia Nature Conservancy Society exhibition hall – a photographic favourite. Built in 1649, the church had its moment of glory with the wedding in 1801of the fabulously rich Count Sheremetev to one of his serfs.
Ulitsa Vorovskovo 5. Tel: 291 2184. Metro: Arbatskaya.

Ancient Russian Culture and Art are on permanent display within.
Novozavodskaya Ulitsa, 10 minutes' walk north from Metro Fili.

KHRAM ROZHDESTVA BOGORODITSIY (Church of the Nativity of the Virgin)
This tiny church was once part of the neighbouring Simonov monastery. When the monastery was part levelled to make way for the vast Dinamo works, the church was somehow left in the middle of the factory grounds. It is one of Moscow's most ancient churches, dating from 1370 and first erected by Russia's patron saint, Sergiy Radonezhskiy.
Ulitsa Vostochnaya 6. Tel: 275 7011. Metro: Avtozavodskaya.

KHRAM SIMEONA STOLNIKA (Church of St Simon Stylites)
It is the juxtaposition of this little church against the monolithic tower blocks of the Novy Arbat that make the building – bare inside after years of service as the

TSERKOV BOLSHOVO VOZNESENIYA (Church of the Grand Ascension)
This monumental church (1840) witnessed the wedding of Alexander Pushkin and was beloved of Tchaikovsky for its marvellous acoustics. The Soviets, vandalised it thoroughly, converting it by turn into a workshop, garage and lightning conductor research laboratory.
Ulitsa Bolshaya Nikitskaya 36. Tel: 202 9878. Metro: Arbatskaya.

TSERKOV NIKOLY V KHAMOVNIKAKH (Church of St Nicholas of the Weavers)
One of Moscow's best-loved – and gaudiest – churches, St Nicholas dates from the 17th century, when it was commissioned by the city's weavers. As eyecatching as the exterior is the decoration inside – preserved because the church remained open during Soviet rule.
Ulitsa Lva Tolstovo 2. Tel: 246 6952. Metro: Park Kultury.

Galleries and Exhibitions

*M*oscow has a wealth of galleries including some, such as the Pushkin Fine Arts Museum, of world-wide reputation. But the city is also at the centre of a boom in contemporary art, as new freedoms of artistic expression have brought an explosion of avant-garde talent.

See English-language press for current listings.

Assyrian portal, oriental grandeur in the Pushkin Fine Arts Museum

A-3 GALEREYA (A-3 Gallery)
One of Moscow's best, this gallery is at the leading edge of the city's modern art scene.
Starokonyushenny Pereulok 39. Tel: 291 8484. Open: 11am–7pm. Closed: Monday. Admission charge. Metro: Smolenskaya.

GALEREYA GROSITSKOVO (Grositskiy Gallery)
Part ethnographer, part art collector, showroom proprietor Konstantin Grositskiy travels on foot between Russia's far-flung villages to find and bring back to Moscow simple handcrafted gems. Their functional elegance puts to shame the crude

Matryoshkas of the flea-market.
Maliy Lavrushinskiy Pereulok 15. Tel: 231 4049. Open: weekdays 10am–6pm. Admission charge. Metro: Tretyakovskaya.

MARS GALEREYA (MARS Gallery)
Situated in a western suburb of Moscow, this gallery has built a reputation as one of the city's foremost exhibition centres of contemporary works. The founders were among those whose exhibitions were famously bulldozed by the authorities in the 1970s (see pages 68–9). Work is regularly on sale and credit cards are accepted.
Malaya Filyovskaya Ulitsa 32. Tel: 146 2029. Open: noon–8pm. Closed: Monday. Free. Metro: Pionerskaya.

MUZEY IZOBRAZITELNYKH ISKUSSTV IM A S PUSHKINA (Pushkin Fine Arts Museum)
While the Pushkin Museum has good collections of classical and Egyptian antiquities and copies of Renaissance sculpture, it is best known for its rich holdings of European painting – especially the French Impressionists – second only to the Hermitage in St

Petersburg (see pages 98–101). The upper floor contains important works by Cézanne, Manet, Monet, Gauguin, Matisse and Picasso (Rooms 17–18 and 21). Earlier European artists, including Rembrandt, Rubens, El Greco and Botticelli, are well represented.

The museum rocked the art world in 1995 when it showed for the first time paintings plundered from private collections by Soviet troops at the end of World War II, including *Carnival* by Goya, Manet's *Portrait of Rosita Maury*, El Greco's *St Bernard*, and *Portrait of Madame Choquet at the Window* by Renoir. Many had been written off as lost masterpieces. Whether the paintings will remain in the museum is a matter of diplomatic debate: the Ambassador of Germany, from where most of the works were taken, first knew of their existence when he received an invitation to the exhibition's opening day and the embassy has since demanded their return.

Ulitsa Volkhonka 12. Tel: 203 9578. Open: 10am–7pm. Closed: Monday. Admission charge. Tours in English are available. Metro: Kropotkinskaya.

The Central Artist's House, home of contemporary Russian art

NOVAYA TRETYAKOVSKAYA GALEREYA (New Tretyakov Gallery)
The back half of the Central Artist's House (see below) hosts temporary exhibitions from the collections of the Tretyakov Gallery proper.

PHOTOTSENTR (Photo Centre)
One of Moscow's most consistently interesting photographic galleries shows regular exhibitions of Russian and some foreign photojournalism.
Gogolevskiy Bulvar 8. Tel: 290 4188. Open: noon–8pm. Closed: Monday. Admission charge. Metro: Kropotkinskaya.

TRETYAKOVSKAYA GALEREYA (Tretyakov Gallery)
See pages 66–7.

TSENTRALNIY DOM KHUDOZHNIKA (Central Artist's House)
This huge building opposite the gates of Gorky Park is Russia's premier exhibition centre of contemporary art from all over the country. The gallery grounds are now the resting place of many of Moscow's revolutionary statues: a kind of communist elephants' graveyard.
Krymskiy Val Ulitsa 10. Tel: 238 9843. Open: daily 11am–9pm. Admission charge. Metro: Park Kultury.

STREET LIFE

'The Russians are in general a very quarrelsome people who assail each other like dogs, with fierce harsh words. Again and again on the streets one sees such quarrels; the old women shout with such fury that he who is unaccustomed to it expects them at any moment to seize each other's hair.' Day-to-day life on the streets of Russia always makes a powerful impression, as it did on this German diplomat writing in the mid-17th century.

As the populations of both cities wrestle with the collapse of old Soviet certainties, be prepared to see almost anything on a stroll down the main thoroughfares of Moscow

The city streets offer a parade of sights – colourful, bizarre and pathetic. Above: Hare Krishna procession in St Petersburg. Left: street musician, Moscow. Opposite above: queueing for scarce goods. Opposite: street cleaner in St Petersburg's Nevskiy Prospekt

tables, while black-robed Orthodox fathers collect funds for the restoration of derelict churches ... It all differs little from the days when a horrified Catherine the Great complained: 'The town is full of symbols of fanaticism, miraculous icons, and convents side by side with thieves and brigands.'

Glittering with the neon lights of mushrooming casinos and nightclubs, the streets are, for some, a place to parade new-found wealth. For others, they are a lifestyle: the homeless – *bomzhi* – used to be rounded up and herded out beyond the city limits. Now no-one has time even for that.

But one thing may never change: the streets themselves. 'I have in my time seen bad roads of all descriptions, and on both sides of the world,' remarked an English visitor in the 19th century. 'But I have never seen any roads in town or country so atrociously bad as the streets of Moscow.'

and St Petersburg. Old women crossing themselves beg for a few roubles from designer-clothed young businessmen ... Shaven-headed Hare Krishna recruits beating tambourines dance past nonplussed drunkards ... Street traders fight for the best spots to set up their

Krasnaya Ploshchad
(Red Square)

*W*itness to holy processions and executions, grandiose military parades and bloody insurrections, the vast, cobbled expanse of Red Square is the spiritual heart of both capital and nation. At the far end, the visitor's eye is drawn by the fantastic cupolas of St Basil's Cathedral, quintessential symbol of Moscow.

A bustling market place in early times, the square saw Ivan the Terrible beg forgiveness for his misdeeds and Peter the Great personally undertake the beheading of his foes. '*Krasnaya*' in old Russian meant 'beautiful' and it is only recently that the square became identified with 'red' communism.
Metro: Ploshchad Revolyutsii.

GUM
Privatised, and officially known as the 'Upper Trading Rows', this glorious shopping arcade opposite the Kremlin is still affectionately known by its Soviet acronym, standing for 'State Department Store'. Completed in 1888, its bridges and balconies afford a bird's-eye view of the post-Soviet shopping frenzy below.

KAZANSKIY SOBOR (The Kazan Cathedral)
Constructed in 1636 in honour of the miraculous 'Mother of God of Kazan' icon that helped rid Muscovy of the Poles, Kazan Cathedral was destroyed by Stalin exactly 300 years later to erect public toilets. Detailed plans were kept in secret, however, and it was rebuilt to be blessed by the Patriarch in late 1993.

LOBNOE MESTO
While the origins of the name are unclear, the history of Muscovy's ancient tribune is dramatic. In 1613, the first of the Romanov dynasty, Mikhail, was here

proclaimed tsar; the leader of the 1682 peasants' revolt, Stenka Razin, was led along the street now bearing his name to be quartered on the site; and Peter the Great reputedly executed the first 10 of the 2,000 rebellious palace guard here in 1698.

MAVZOLEY V I LENINA (Lenin's Mausoleum)
See page 48.

MININ-POZHARSKIY
The statue outside St Basil's depicts the Nizhny Novgorod butcher Minin persuading Prince Pozharskiy to lead the army of liberation on Moscow and drive out the occupying Poles. The work was commissioned in a flush of nationalism following the defeat of Napoleon and completed in 1818. Reliefs show the collection of funds in Nizhny Novgorod and the final surrender of the Poles in 1612.

SPASSKAYA (The Saviour's Tower)
Broadcast on the radio at daybreak, midday and midnight, the bells of the Saviour's Tower, erected in 1491, defined the Soviet worker's day. Under Stalin, the *Internationale* chimed out over Red Square. The small tower alongside was built for Ivan the Terrible so that he could watch executions in comfort.

VASILIYA BLAZHENNOVO KHRAM (St Basil's Cathedral)
Napoleon referred to it as 'that Mosque' and stabled his horses there. Whatever one's taste, there is no denying the motley splendour of the Cathedral of the Intercession of the Virgin, better known as St Basil's after the 'holy fool' famed for his denunciation of Ivan the Terrible and buried in one of the chapels.

Ivan decreed work on the building to begin following the capture of the Khanate of Kazan; legend has it that he had the architects' eyes put out on completion in 1555 to prevent them creating anything more beautiful.

The central chapel reaches a height of 57m and the surrounding eight are built to strict geometric design. The exterior was originally white and gold, the present vivid colour scheme being added in the 17th century. The interior is more understated, but it is well worth wandering the convoluted corridors to see the frescos and icons.

GUM, home of Mammon, confronts St Basil's Cathedral, famous repository of Orthodox faith

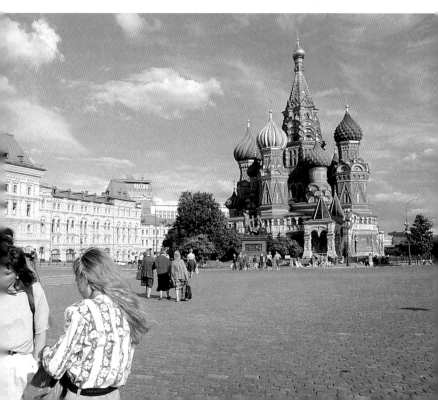

Kreml
(The Kremlin)

*A*ll highways in Russia lead to the gates of this, the very hub of imperial and Soviet might. To the visitor it is an unnerving place, where the sublime beauty of the medieval cathedral coexists with the terror of the torture tower.

The Kremlin dates back to 1156, shortly after Moscow was founded. In 1367, Prince Dmitri Donskoy pulled down the wooden bailey and erected limestone battlements. These in turn were replaced at the end of the 15th century by vast walls, up to 19m high and 6.5m in width.

CATHEDRALS
The heart of the Kremlin is the flag-stoned expanse of Sobornaya Ploshchad (Cathedral Square), the spiritual focus of

Imperial Russia. Site of royal weddings, coronations and christenings, it is the final resting place of many of the tsars.

ARKHANGELSKIY SOBOR (Cathedral of the Archangel Michael)
Dedicated to the patron of the Princes of Muscovy, the cathedral was built in 1508. A team of over 100 artists from all over the kingdom were enlisted to paint the frescos of ancient Russian warriors. Several early tsars are entombed here including Mikhail, first of the Romanovs, and Ivan the Terrible (the latter out of sight behind the iconostasis).

BLAGOVESHCHENSKIY SOBOR (Cathedral of the Annunciation)
Built in 1489, the tsars' private church, paved with jasper and capped with nine cupolas, contains 16th-century biblical frescos and one of Russia's most precious iconostases. From the chapel to the right Ivan the Terrible, forbidden by Orthodox law to enter the church itself, watched proceedings through a partition.

TSERKOV RIZPOLOZHERIYA AND PATRIARSHIY PALATY (Cathedral of the Deposition of the Robe and Patriarch's Palace)
Serving as a private chapel, this smaller church is linked to the Patriarch's Palace

The Cathedral of the Annunciation contains icons by the great master Andrei Rublev

(1655). It is decorated with 17th-century frescos and now holds a small woodcarving museum.

The palace contains an exhibition of gold and silver ware and ornate church vestments. Most of the exhibits are from Kremlin monasteries destroyed by Stalin.

USPENSKIY SOBOR (Cathedral of the Dormition)

The cathedral (1479) houses the tombs of all the patriarchs up to 1700. In 1812 Napoleon stabled his horses here. And in 1989 it witnessed the first religious service in the Kremlin since 1918.

KREML PLAN

Moskovskiy Universitet
UL BOLSHAYA NIKITSKAYA
Moskovskiy Universitet
OKHOTNIY RYAD
Manezh
MANEZHNAYA
ULITSA
Aleksandrovskiy Sad
Kutafya
Aleksandrovskiy Sad
MANEZHNAYA
Aleksandrovskiy Sad
Kommendatskaya
Oruzheynaya
BOROVITSKAYA PLOSHCHAD
Borovitskaya
Vodovoznaya

MANEZHNAYA PLOSHCHAD
Uglovaya Arsenalnaya
Memorial Mogila Neizvestnovo Soldata
Obelisk
Srednyaya Arsenalnaya
Arsenal
Aleksandrovskiy Sad
Troitskaya
Tserkov Rizopolozheniya
Dvorets Syezdov
Poteshniy Dvorets
Teremnoy Dvorets
Patriarshiy Palaty
Oruzheynaya Palata

Istoricheskiy Muzey
Nikolskaya
Kreml
Senate
Tsar Pushka
Sobor Dvenadtsati Apostolov
Uspenskiy Sobor
SOBORNAYA PLOSHCHAD
Granovitiy Dvorets
Bolshoy Kremlevskiy Dvorets
Blagoveshchenskiy Sobor
Taynitskaya
Blagoveshchenskaya

Monetniy Dvor
Kazanskiy Sobor
KRASNAYA PLOSHCHAD
Mavzoley V I Lenina
Prezidium Verkhovnovo Soveta
Tsar Kolokol
Kolokolnya Ivan Velikiy
Arkhangelskiy Sobor
1-Bezymyannaya
2-Bezymyannaya

Bogoyavlenskiy Monastyr
PROEZD SAPUNOVA
GUM
ULITSA ILINKA
Lobnoe Mesto
Spasskaya
Minin-Pozharskiy
Vasiliya Blazhennogo Khram
Tsarskaya
Nabatnaya
Konstantin-Yelena
Beklemishevskaya
Petrovskaya
NABEREZHNAYA
KREMLEVSKAYA
Moskva
NABEREZHNAYA MORISA TOREZA
FALEYEVSKIY PERELIOK
BOLSHOY KAMENNIY MOST

0   100   200 m

OTHER SIGHTS
KOLOKOLNYA IVAN VELIKIY
(Ivan the Great Bell Tower)

For long the tallest structure in Moscow, the 81m-high Ivan the Great Bell Tower (1600) dominates Cathedral Square. The tower commands a 40km view across the capital yet its foundations are little more than 4m deep. It was initially part of Tserkov Ioana Lestvichnika (Church of St John Climacus). Today 18 of the original 36 bells remain.

ORUZHEYNAYA PALATA
(The Armoury)

One of the high points of a Kremlin tour is the fabulous wealth on show in the Armoury building. There's a stunning exhibition of treasures such as the battle helmet of Mikhail, first of the Romanov dynasty and the ivory throne of Ivan the Terrible. An additional fee gains entrance to the State Diamond Fund, a collection of some of the world's most fantastic gemstones. Seize the chance to see the collection of jewelled Easter eggs created by Carl Fabergé for the tsar's family.

The Armoury is closest to the Borovitskaya Gates entrance.

Right: the mighty Tsar Bell, too heavy to hoist.
Below: the Great Kremlin Palace

TOWERS

Of the Kremlin's 20 towers, the Konstantin-Yelena Tower was a torture chamber and the Blagoveshchenskaya (Annunciation) Tower was used as a prison. The small Tsarskaya (Tsar's) Tower beside the Spasskaya Gates used to be a wooden pavilion from which Ivan the Terrible watched executions on Red Square. The rotating red stars atop each of the towers, made from Ural mountains ruby, were erected in 1937 in place of the tsarist two-headed eagle.

TSAR KOLOKOL AND TSAR PUSHKA (Tsar Bell and Cannon)

The Tsar Bell – at 210 tonnes the world's largest – was cast in 1735 but proved too heavy to hoist and was never rung. Similarly, the Tsar Cannon, intended to defend the Kremlin's Spasskaya Gates, was never fired. Cast in 1586, it boasts an 890mm calibre.

Kremlin open: 10am–5pm except Thursday. Tel: 921 4720. Admission charge. Tickets for separate sights sold at Kutafya tower in the Alexander Gardens. Metro: Aleksandrovskiy Sad

---

The following are normally open only to special tour groups; individuals must apply to the Kremlin Commandant. Tel: 224 3563/6685. (See Practical Guide page 189 for tour agencies.)

BOLSHOY KREMLEVSKIY DVORETS (Great Kremlin Palace)

Overlooking the river, the tsars' Moscow residence was built for Nicholas I in 1849. The royal apartments have been preserved in pre-revolutionary splendour. Communist leaders lay in state in the Giorgiesvskiy Zal (St George's Hall).

DVORETS SYEZDOV (Palace of Congresses)

The key speeches of Gorbachev's *perestroika* were delivered in the 6,000-seat auditorium of this fiercely modern building (1961) also used as a second venue for the Bolshoy opera and ballet.

GRANOVITAYA DVORETS (Palace of Facets)

The squat Palace of Facets (1491) once formed part of the Grand Duke of Muscovy's stone residence. It was later used as a banqueting hall and for the celebrated transvestite balls held by the wildly extravagant Empress Elizabeth (reigned 1741–61).

PREZIDIUM VERKHOVNOVO SOVETA, SENATE AND ARSENAL (Praesidium of the Supreme Soviet, the Senate and the Arsenal)

To the left as you look from the Palace of Congresses is the state Arsenal, built in the early 18th century to Peter the Great's plan. Over 800 captured French cannon ring the building's pediment

In the centre stands the former Senate building (1787), once headquarters of the Soviet government and now housing the presidential administration. Lenin's offices are preserved within in a special museum (see page 49). To the right is the former Praesidium of the Supreme Soviet.

TEREMNOY DVORETS (Terem Palace)

Built originally for Tsar Mikhail Romanov, this is perhaps the Kremlin's most spectacular building. The interior seems to owe more to fairytale Baghdad than 17th-century Moscow with its low vaulted ceilings, lavish gilding, ornate tilework and stained-glass windows.

Lenin's Moscow

*C*hanges in the political climate have seen the axing of funds allocated to maintaining Russia's Lenin industry: where once you could not take two steps without being reminded of the 1917 revolution's mastermind, Lenin is slowly slipping off Moscow's map. Street names are reverting to their ancient originals and the huge Central Lenin Museum on Ploshchad Revolyutsii, which boasted over 50 million visitors, has been returned to the city authorities. Still, there remain a few spots that shed light on one of history's greatest, if most infamous, figures.

MAVZOLEY V I LENINA
(Lenin's Mausoleum)

A week after his death, Lenin's wife Krupskaya wrote to *Pravda* imploring: 'Do not build memorials to him or palaces to his name. Do not organise pompous ceremonies in his memory.' Her pleas went unanswered and the result is the granite and porphyry ziggurat that has since seen over 80 million of the faithful and the curious.

Bedecked in a polka dot bow tie,

Lenin is maintained in his crystal sarcophagus by a computer-controlled ventilation system and a yearly bathing with a chemical cocktail. The honour guard at the gates was abolished by Yeltsin, but changing political fortunes have put on hold plans to clear the site. Thousands of old communists still gather here on 22 April to celebrate their idol's birthday.

The Kremlin wall behind the building is the ex-USSR's principal necropolis. Here, with Stalin and other Bolshevik luminaries, lie Yuri Gagarin, the first man in space, and the American chronicler of

The red granite and porphyry mausoleum where Lenin's preserved body still draws the faithful

VLADIMIR ILYICH ULYANOV – 'LENIN' (1870–1924)

Born in the southern city of Simbirsk (now Ulyanovsk), Lenin took up radical politics in earnest after his brother was executed for attempting to assassinate the tsar. Much of his life was spent exiled in Europe, quarrelling in cafés with the many other émigré socialists. He looked 'more like a provincial grocer than a leader of men' according to one British agent, but what marked Lenin out from the rest was his genius for seizing the moment.

Smuggled into Russia by the Germans during World War 1, he and his tiny 'Bolshevik' ('majority') party grabbed power in more of a farcical coup than a revolution. As his partner Leon Trotsky remarked, 'Power was lying in the streets.' Lenin simply picked it up.

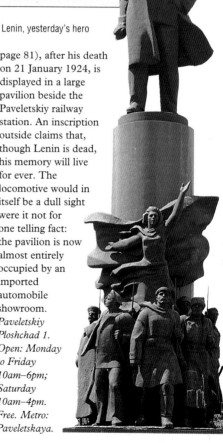

Lenin, yesterday's hero

the Revolution, John Reed. *Krasnaya Ploshchad. Tel: 224 5115. Open: Tuesday to Thursday and Saturday 10am–1pm; Sunday 10am–3pm. Free. Metro: Ploshchad Revolyutsii, Okhotniy Ryad. Bags and cameras must be checked in at the Historical Museum.*

MUZEY KABINET-KVARTIRA LENINA V KREMLYE (Lenin's Kremlin Apartment)

The Senate building in the Kremlin (see page 47) contains the rooms occupied by Lenin after the Revolution. Once a sanctuary reserved for especially important foreign guests, the apartment can now be visited by anyone with special permission. The progress of the Civil War is marked with flags on a map hanging on the study wall, and notepaper and envelopes on the desk are headed 'Chairman of the Council of People's Commissars'.

Access involves a request to the Kremlin Commandant. For details, tel: 224 3563/6685.

TRAURNY POEZD LENINA (Lenin's Funeral Train)

The train which transported Lenin's body from his country estate Gorki (see page 81), after his death on 21 January 1924, is displayed in a large pavilion beside the Paveletskiy railway station. An inscription outside claims that, though Lenin is dead, his memory will live for ever. The locomotive would in itself be a dull sight were it not for one telling fact: the pavilion is now almost entirely occupied by an imported automobile showroom. *Paveletskiy Ploshchad 1. Open: Monday to Friday 10am–6pm; Saturday 10am–4pm. Free. Metro: Paveletskaya.*

LUBYANKA (The Lubyanka)

'I have learned how faces fell to bone,
how under the eyelids terror lurks,
How suffering inscribes on cheeks the
hard lines of its cuneiform texts ...'
The poem *Requiem* by Anna
Akhmatova (1888–1966) vividly recalls
the systematic repression of Stalin's
purges whose nerve-centre was the dour
building dominating former Dzerzhinsky
Square, known simply as 'The
Lubyanka'.
Lubyanskaya Ploshchad. Metro: Lubyanka.

The notorious Lubyanka. Many who passed
through its portals never saw freedom again

Red Terror

Lenin established the KGB's forerunner
– the CheKa – in the Rossiya Insurance
building on Lubyanskaya Ploshchad.
Pravda outlined his policy of terror in
1918: 'Do not demand incriminating
evidence to prove that the prisoner has
opposed the Soviet government ... Your
first duty is to ask him to which class he
belongs ... This question should decide
the fate of the prisoner.'

The Purges

Successor organisations like the NKVD
became the instrument of Stalin's
crackdown on real and imaginary Party
opposition in the 1930s. Victims
disappeared through the back gates on
Furkasovskiy Pereulok; torture and
execution took place in the courtyard and
basement. Between 5 and 7 million were
arrested in the Great Purge of 1937–8
alone, most ending up – and dying – in
the Gulag Archipelago of prison camps.

As the headquarters of the KGB, the
Lubyanka was, in 1991, the scene of
demonstrations toppling the statue of
CheKa founder, Felix Dzerzhinskiy –
and symbolically the Soviet regime.

THE METRO

Moscow's metro system is reputedly the
world's most efficient but rates as a
'must' among the capital's tourist sights
for the less prosaic reason that many
stations are architecturally as stunning as
anything on offer above ground.
*Open: daily 6am–1am. See pages 26–7 for
Metro map and page 186 for public
transport details.*

Underground Palace

At 7am on 15 May 1935, Mr Lakyshev
of the Red Proletariat factory bought a
ticket at Sokolniki station and became

the first of over 77 billion passengers to ride Moscow's celebrated metro.

Komsomolskaya station. Inset: metro portrait of Gorky

The metro was planned by Stalin as a showpiece of communist engineering, capable of transporting the city's workers rapidly and in the lap of socialist luxury. The older stations are the most impressive, heavily decorated with marble, stucco, and crystal. Komsomolskaya (Circle Line) is among the most lavish, while the bronzes of square-jawed workers and buxom farmers' wives at Ploshchad Revolyutsii are unforgettable. Also impressive are Mayakovskaya, Kievskaya (Circle Line), Novokuznetskaya and Novoslobodskaya.

Wartime metro

Constructed to double as air-raid shelters, many of the stations are extremely deep underground. In 1941, Stalin addressed deputies in Mayakovskaya on the anniversary of the Revolution and had an office at Chistiye Prudy in the Air Defence Command outpost – reached by a secret door behind the bust of Kirov.

Besides the metro, Moscow is riddled with other tunnels. Some link with the former KGB's headquarters while those beneath the White House and the Kremlin are reportedly wide enough to drive a car down.

SOME STATISTICS
Every day, 506 escalators (137,814 steps) at 150 stations carry over eight million passengers to 7,840 trains that travel 244km of track and consume four million kWh of electricity.

THE RESURRECTION OF RELIGION

After decades of Soviet intimidation, the clatter of stonemasons' chisels, the shine of newly-gilded cupolas and the low tones of the Orthodox liturgy issuing from candlelit churches throughout Moscow and St Petersburg are sure signs of a massive rebirth of religion.

Perestroika gave the impetus. In exchange for church support of his reforms, Gorbachev authorised mass celebrations on the 1988 millennium of Grand Prince Vladimir's – and with it, Russia's – baptism into the Christian faith. It was a long way from the hostility of the Soviets to the 'opium of the people'.

The church had been a mainstay of the tsarist regime, expressed in the slogan 'Orthodoxy, Autocracy, Nationality', and the Bolsheviks sought ruthlessly to uproot it, fearing it would become a centre of opposition.

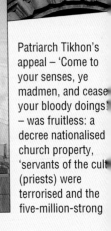

Patriarch Tikhon's appeal – 'Come to your senses, ye madmen, and cease your bloody doings' – was fruitless: a decree nationalised church property, 'servants of the cult' (priests) were terrorised and the five-million-strong

Paradise regained for the Russian Orthodox Church: atheism is out and religious worship approved once more

'Godless League' organised aeroplane trips for the peasants to prove that God did not live in the clouds.

Once himself a seminary student, Stalin energetically furthered the destruction, pausing only for a temporary truce for the sake of wartime morale. Khrushchev and Brezhnev took up the slack – of the 848 Moscow churches in 1917, only 78 functioned and more than half were destroyed by 1990.

The church survived, but at a cost. The priesthood is split between collaborators and those who languished in labour camps while the Patriarchy, like any other ex-Soviet monopolist, struggles to cope with the free market flood of imported evangelists.

The incongruous sight of politicians of left and right, most of them card-carrying communists a few years ago, crossing themselves for the TV cameras, shows that the church again occupies its traditional place at the right hand of Russian government.

Monasteries and Convents

*B*efore the Revolution, Russia's 5,000 or more monasteries and convents were the focal points of traditional life. Many of the most splendid were in Moscow. Of those that survived the communist onslaught, some remain in ruins or converted into factories and workshops, but many are now slowly returning to life, their newly-gilded churches recalling past glories.

DANILOVSKIY MONASTYR
(Danilov Monastery)
Moscow's most ancient monastery dates from 1282 and is named after its founder, Prince Daniel, son of Alexander Nevsky. After use as a juvenile delinquents' prison, it resumed its role as the headquarters of the Orthodox Patriarchate during *perestroika* (hence its spruce appearance). The oldest church within is the 17th-century Church of the Holy Fathers, containing Daniel's relics, and packed with worshippers on church festivals. Beggars throng the Church of Simeon Stylites at the monastery entrance – giving to the poor is a central element of the Orthodox faith, which is observed punctiliously today.

Entrance is free but, as in all Russian religious buildings, modest dress and respectful behaviour is expected.
Danilovskiy Val 22. Tel: 955 6787. Metro: Tulskaya.

DONSKOY MONASTYR
(Don Monastery)
Patriarch Tikhon was kept under arrest by the Bolsheviks in the monastery's Old Cathedral where his tomb now lies. The Don Monastery is also the resting place of many of Moscow's aristocrats, including the wealthy Golitsyn family who are buried in the Church of the Archangel Michael in the monastery grounds.

The oldest buildings and fortress walls date from the 16th century when the monastery was founded by Boris Godunov in honour of the Don Mother of God icon, whose miraculous powers were believed to have helped defeat the Crimean Tartars. The original icon is now in the Tretyakov Gallery (see pages 66–7). Today the monastery is once again operative.
Donskaya Ploshchad 1. Tel: 952 1646. Metro: Shabolovskaya.

NOVODEVICHIY MONASTYR
(Convent of the New Maidens)
Peter the Great banished his sister Sophia to a cell in this breathtakingly beautiful ensemble, for alleged participation in a revolt. The Austrian ambassador watched in horror as the culprits were tortured and hung before her window: 'Nobody will easily believe how lamentable were their Cries and Howls, unless he has well weighed their Excruciations and the Greatness of their Tortures.'

The convent's most notable buildings are the red-brick bell tower (1690) and the central Smolensk Cathedral (1525) containing stunning frescos and Sophia's tomb. A number of exhibitions occupy the lesser buildings.

The adjoining cemetery is Moscow's most prestigious and the site of the graves of the writers Anton Chekhov and Nikolai Gogol, film director Sergei

Iconostasis in Donskoy Monastery church

Eisenstein and – most famously – Communist Party General Secretary Nikita Khrushchev, removed from power in disgrace and hence denied a plot in the Kremlin Wall (see page 48). You can buy a guide to the cemetery at the entrance gates.

In good weather, the view of the complex from across the lake is unforgettable. *Novodevichiy Proezd 1. Convent – tel: 246 8526; cemetery – tel: 246 6614. Open: 10am–6pm. Closed: Monday. Admission charge. Metro: Sportivnaya.*

NOVOSPASSKIY MONASTYR (Novospasskiy Monastery)

This pretty monastery (1490) on a lakeside hill by the Moskva river, has a sinister past. It has been a children's prison, a furniture factory, a sobering-up centre for arrested female drunks, and a base of the NKVD secret police, forerunner of the KGB. Summary executions were carried out in the monastery yards – mass graves of the victims were discovered in the banks beneath the monastery towers after the complex was surrendered to the church in 1991.

The central Cathedral of the Transfiguration (1647), built as the family church of the Romanov dynasty, now holds services again. *Krestyanskaya Ploshchad 10. Tel: 276 9570. Metro: Proletarskaya.*

Museums

*M*oscow's streets are dotted with museums covering every imaginable topic. The following is only a small selection of what's on offer.

BORODINSKAYA BITVA PANORAMA (Borodino Battle Panorama)
Desperate Russian resistance scotched Napoleon's expectations of an easy victory on the fields of Borodino in 1812, a battle celebrated in this vast panorama. The huge losses suffered on both sides made Borodino a symbol of Russia's struggle against foreign invasion.
Kutuzovskiy Prospekt 38. Tel: 148 1965. Soon to reopen after repairs. Metro: Kutuzovskaya.

DOM ROMANOVIKH (Romanov House)
Built by the grandfather of Tsar Mikhail, the first of the Romanov dynasty, this elegant city residency has been restored as a museum of 16th- and 17th-century aristocratic life.
Ulitsa Varvarka 10. Tel: 298 3706. Open: 10am–5pm (Tuesday and Wednesday 11am–6pm). Closed: first Monday of the

Scene from the Borodino Battle Panorama

month. Admission charge. Metro: Ploshchad Revolyutsii.

MUZEY DEKORATIVNO-PRIKLADNOVO ISKUSSTVA (Applied Arts Museum)
A stunning exhibition of traditional arts including jewellery, ceramics and superb-quality lacquered boxes.
Ulitsa Delegatskaya 3. Tel: 923 7725. Open: 10am–6pm. Closed: Friday and the last Thursday of the month. Admission charge. Metro: Tsvetnoy Bulvar.

MUZEY DREVNERUSSKOI KULTURY I ISKUSSTVA IMENI ANDREYA RUBLYOVA (Rublyov Museum of Ancient Russian Culture and Art)
You will find a rich display of religious art displayed in the Andronnikov Monastery and can also visit the museum's adjoining restoration studios.
Andronyevskaya Ploshchad 10. Tel: 278 1467. Open: 10am–5.30pm. Closed: Wednesday. Admission charge. Metro: Ploshchad Ilyicha.

MUZEY ISTORII REKONSTRUKTSII GORODA MOSKVY (Museum of the History of Moscow)
The systematic destruction of religion in the capital is but one of the themes illustrated by this collection of prints,

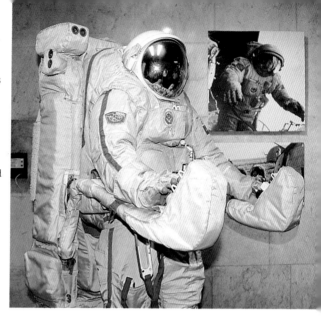

Space-walk kit in Moscow's Space Travel Museum

lithographs and archaeological bits and pieces relating to Moscow's chequered architectural history and occupying what was once the Church of St John the Evangelist. *Novaya Ploshchad 12. Tel: 924 8490. Open: 10am–6pm, Friday and Saturday 11am–7pm). Closed: Monday. Admission charge. Metro: Lubyanka.*

MUZEY IZOBRAZITELNYKH ISKUSSTV IM A S PUSHKINA (Pushkin Fine Arts Museum)
See pages 38–9

MUZEY KOSMONAVTOV (Space Travel Museum)
Situated beneath the massive titanium rocket monument at VDNKh (see page 63), the museum contains a modest collection of space hardware ranging from early satellites to the space suits of the first cosmonaut, Yuri Gagarin, and a number of the dogs (now stuffed) blasted into orbit prior to Gagarin's flight. *Pervaya Ostankinskaya Ulitsa 41/9. Tel: 286 3714. Open: 10am–7pm. Closed: Monday. Admission charge. Metro: VDNKh.*

MUZEY MINISTERSTVA VNUTRENNIKH DYEL (Interior Ministry Museum)
Devoted to Russia's police or 'militsia', this fascinating museum includes exhibits as up-to-date as the clubs and lumps of

masonry wielded by hardline demonstrators during the October 1993 uprising, as well as a gruesome photo display illustrating the hunt for the infamous serial killer Andrei Chikatillo. *Ulitsa Seleznyovskaya 11. Tel: 258 0135. Open: Tuesday to Saturday 10am–4pm, groups only. Admission charge. Metro: Novoslobodskaya. Call ahead to book tour.*

MUZEY REVOLYUTSII (Museum of the Revolution)
Rather than close down what was once a centrepiece of tourist-orientated propaganda, the curators have produced an even-handed tour through the convulsions of Russia's revolutionary past. The exhibits range from bold communist posters to a tableau of the barricades of 1991 as the Soviet Union drew its final gasps for survival. *Tverskaya Ulitsa 21. Tel: 299 5217. Open: Tuesday and Thursday to Saturday 10am–5.30pm; Wednesday 11am–6.30pm; Sunday 10am–4.30pm. Closed: Monday. Admission charge. Metro: Tverskaya.*

Armed Forces Museum: part of the Soviet armoury that menaced the West during the Cold War

MUZEY VOORUZHONNYKH SIL (Armed Forces Museum)

Full of the hardware with which Soviet leaders threatened to 'bury the west', this excellent museum also contains memorabilia of the Red Army's most famous victories. The remains of Gary Power's U2 spyplane, shot down in 1960, are here.

Ulitsa Sovetskoy Armii 2. Tel: 281 1880. Open: Tuesday and Friday to Sunday, 10am–5 pm; Wednesday and Thursday noon–7pm. Closed: Monday and the penultimate Tuesday of the month. Metro: Prospekt Mira.

POLITEKHINICHESKIY MUZEY (Polytechnical Museum)

A little rusted and loose at the seams, the displays on the achievements of Soviet science and industry are still worth a visit on a rainy day. A good 50 per cent of the button-operated exhibits are still in working order.

Novaya Ploshchad 3/4. Tel: 923 0756.

Open: 10am–5.30pm. Closed: Monday and the last Thursday of the month. Metro: Lubyanka.

HOUSE MUSEUMS

Moscow is littered with museums in homes of the great and the good. Clocks are stopped at the time of death and the rooms and effects preserved as found. With shifting financial priorities, many have been closed, but those dedicated to the following should survive:

SERGEI EISENSTEIN

The study of the Soviet Union's greatest cinematographer (1898–1948), famed especially for *The Battleship Potemkin*, *Alexander Nevsky* and *Ivan the Terrible*, and his stunning but entirely imaginary depiction of the storming of the Winter Palace in 1917, is a worthy destination for cinema buffs.

Kabinet S N Eyzenshteyna – Smolenskaya Ulitsa 10. Tel: 241 8030. Open: by arrangement. Metro: Smolenskaya.

MAXIM GORKY

Despite his serious misgivings about the 1917 revolution, Gorky (1868–1936) was lionised by the state as a pillar of proletarian literature and promoted as a model for young Soviet writers. Coaxed back from emigration and disillusion in 1928, Gorky lived in a wonderful example of Russian avant-garde architecture till his death, rumoured to be at Stalin's prompting.

Muzey Kvartira im Gorkovo – Ulitsa Malaya Nikitskaya 6/2. Tel: 290 0535. Open: Wednesday, Friday, Saturday and Sunday noon–6.30pm; Thursday 10am–4.30pm. Closed: Monday and Tuesday. Admission charge. Metro: Arbatskaya.

ALEXANDER PUSHKIN

The reverence reserved for Russia's premier poet (1799–1837) – almost as for a saint – far exceeds that of the English for Shakespeare and the Germans for Goethe. It is evidenced in the hushed awe with which local visitors pore over the author's collected manuscripts, jottings and possessions gathered in two museums, the second of which was for a short time Pushkin's home.

Literaturniy Muzey A S Pushkina, Ulitsa Prechistenka 12. Tel: 201 3256. Open: Friday to Sunday 10am–6pm, Wednesday and Thursday 11am–7pm. Metro: Kropotinskaya. Dom Muzey A S Pushkina, Arbat 53. Tel: 241 9295. Open: Wednesday to Sunday 11am–5pm. Metro: Smolenskaya.

LEV TOLSTOY

The life, works and philosophy of the grand old man of Russian literature (1828–1910) are celebrated in two Moscow museums. Despite Tolstoy's espousal in later life of such doctrines as vegetarianism and pacifism, his stature was such that even the strict censors of communist aesthetics were forced to leave untouched his works and memory. The Muzey-Usadba Lva Tolstovo, a timbered house where Tolstoy lived between 1882 and 1901 is especially evocative.

Muzey L N Tolstovo, Ulitsa Prechistenka 11. Tel: 202 2190. Open: Tuesday to Sunday 11am–5pm. Metro: Kropotinskaya. Muzey-Usadba Lva Tolstovo, Ulitsa Lva Tolstovo 21. Tel: 246 9444. Open: Tuesday to Sunday 10am–6pm (summer), 10am–4pm (winter). Closed: 1st Friday of the month. Metro: Park Kultury.

VIKTOR VASNETSOV

One of the leaders of the Wanderers' artistic movement at the turn of the century, Vasnetsov (1848–1926) is still much loved for his nostalgic renditions of Russia's mythical past.

Dom-Muzey Khudozhnika V M Vasnetsova, Vasnetsova Pereulok 13. Tel: 281 1329. Open: Wednesday to Sunday 10am–5pm. Closed: last Thursday of the month. Metro: Sukharevskaya.

Tolstoy's desk, preserved in the Tolstoy Estate Museum (Muzey-Usadba Lvo Tolstovo)

THE ARTISTIC EXPLOSION

In the later 19th and early 20th centuries, Russia was gripped by a momentous revolution in the arts which paralleled the turbulent atmosphere of the times. The spirit was one of experiment, a true *fin de siècle* rejection of outmoded doctrines and dusty prejudices.

In 1863, exasperated by its enforced adherence to classical subjects, 14 artists walked out of the St Petersburg Academy of Arts and formed their own group, known as 'The Wanderers' – *Peredvizhniki* – for their travelling exhibitions. Their work dealt innovatively with social issues, epitomised by the searching pictorial parables of Ilya Repin.

Artists were now being supported by Russia's growing class of businessmen, like the railway magnate Savva Mamontov (see page 80) and the merchant Pavel Tretyakov, whose collection of Russian art forms the heart of the Tretyakov Gallery (see pages 66–7).

The 'World of Art' – *Mir Iskusstva* – movement at the turn of the century was driven by the impresario Sergei Diaghilev, whose aim was to 'exalt Russian art in the eyes of the west'. Members such as Alexander Benois, Leon Bakst, and Valentin Serov not only galvanised Russian impressionism and art nouveau, but also designed sets and costumes for Diaghilev, whose Ballets Russes took Europe by storm. The inspired choreography of Michel Fokine and breathtaking dancing of Anna Pavlova and Vaslav Nijinsky, combined with the extraordinary scores of Igor Stravinsky's *Firebird* and *Rite of Spring*, revolutionised ballet.

The Moscow Art Theatre sprang to prominence with the plays of Anton Chekhov and their interpretation by Konstantin Stanislavsky, whose concentration on naturalness gained world-wide renown as the Stanislavsky Method.

Throughout the years surrounding the 1917 Revolution Russian artists were the undisputed leaders of the avant-garde. Movements mushroomed: Primitivism, Rayonnism, Futurism, Supremacism, Constructivism ...

This page: Nijinsky in *Giselle*, 1910.
Opposite: Pavlova as the Dying Swan

The poet of the Revolution, Vladimir Mayakovsky declared: 'We do not need a dead mausoleum of art where dead works are worshipped, but a living factory of the human spirit.' His contemporaries

Above: the great bass Chaliapin. Above right: portrait of Diaghilev

followed his lead, committing themselves wholeheartedly to the great communist experiment which, by the 1930s, had silenced them all.

Ostankino

*P*ainstaking restoration is slowly returning to its former glory the 18th-century summer estate of Count Nikolai Sheremetev, one of Russia's richest and most cultured noblemen. Sadly, much of the property remains closed to the public, but the nearby Ostankino TV tower and the Tekhnopark fully justify a trip out from the centre of town.

OSTANKINSKIY KREPOSTNOI TEATR (Ostankino Theatre)

During Ostankino's heyday, the road from Moscow was lit at night by braziers for those invited to the count's legendary soirées, the focus of which was his famous Serf Theatre.

The daughter of a serf blacksmith, Praskovya Kovalyova-Zhemchugova took to the stage at the age of 11. Breaking all the taboos of high society, Count Sheremetev fell in love with her and freed her from bondage. Catherine the Great forbade the relationship, but on her death Sheremetev prevailed on her son Paul I and the couple were married in 1801. Praskovya died two years later of tuberculosis: the Sklifosovskiy Hospital for the Poor in Moscow was founded in her memory.

The theatre hall is in the main body of the building . Built entirely out of wood, the palace suffers dreadfully from damp and the theatre itself is presently closed to the public.

ITALIANSKIY PAVILION (Italian Pavilion)

The theatre is flanked by two antechambers, the Italian and Egyptian Pavilions, the first of which is open to visitors. The hand-printed wallpaper, gilded woodwork, and stucco ornamentation hint at the luxurious premises enjoyed by the count's privileged guests.

OSTANKINSKAYA TELEBASHNYA (Ostankino TV Tower)

At 540m the world's second-tallest freestanding tower after Toronto's CN tower, the Ostankino TV mast was also the scene of the most vicious gunfire during the uprising of October 1993 (note the pockmarks in the nearby trees). Come here for an unrivalled bird's-eye view of the city – bring your passport and book a place on one of

Ostankino TV Tower

The lovely Ostankino Theatre, within the 18th-century palace of Count Nikolai Sheremetev

Ostankino Palace – tel: 283 4645.
Open: May to September, 10am–5pm
except Monday. Closed in damp
weather. Admission charge. Metro:
VDNKh, then bus or trolleybus down
Ulitsa Akademika Korolyova to the lake.

the daily tours.
*Tel: 282 2038, 282 2293. Tours run
9am–7pm except Monday, with the option
of eating in the revolving restaurant. The
administrative building is located on
Novomoskovskaya Ulitsa. Trolleybus 13
from metro VDNKh takes you there directly.*

TEKHNOPARK (All-Russian Exhibition Centre)

This grandiose park was formerly the
Exhibition of Economic Achievements, a
Soviet Disney World displaying a
fantastically sanitised version of
communist reality. Square-jawed
proletarians stand over the monumental
gates to 2 sq km of kitsch pavilions once
devoted to such Soviet staples as
'Metallurgy', 'Atomic Power',
'Education of the Peoples' and 'Grain'.

Today commercialism has taken over:
in the Cosmos Pavilion, the Apollo-
Soyuz docking craft have been shoved
aside to accommodate a showroom of
BMWs and Harley-Davidsons.
*Open: daily 9am–10pm. Free. Metro:
VDNKh).*

TSERKOV TROITSY (Church of the Trinity)

Overlooking the estate's artificial lake,
the Church of the Trinity (1692) was
built by a serf architect on the site of a
small wooden church. Limestone
decorates the five-domed brick structure
whose chief glory is the intricately carved
wooden iconostasis. The palace grounds
to the west consist of woods and a fair.

Squares

*E*ach of the squares described below offers its own focus of interest. With the exception of Red Square and Theatre Square, site of the imposing Bolshoy Theatre, none perhaps merits a special visit, but all of them are essential crossroads of Moscow urban life.

KOMSOMOLSKAYA PLOSHCHAD
(Komsomol Square)
'Komsomol' was the abbreviation of the League of Young Communists, whose members helped build the palatial metro station beneath your feet.

Above ground, equally memorable is the architecture of the railway termini surrounding the square. Yaroslavskiy Vokzal (Yaroslavl Station), start of the grand Trans-Siberian railway (and adjoining the Leningrad terminus) was built in Russian fairytale style by Fyodor Shekhtel in 1902–4, while the exuberant Kazanskiy Vokzal (Kazan Station) is the work of Aleksei Shchusev, better known for designing Lenin's Mausoleum (see page 48).

Between the stations stands the Leningrad Hotel, one of seven 'wedding cake' buildings constructed to Stalin's taste in the 1940s and '50s.
Metro: Komsomolskaya.

KRASNAYA PLOSHCHAD
(Red Square)
See pages 42–3.

LUBYANSKAYA PLOSHCHAD
(Lubyanka Square)
The square is dominated by the Lubyanka (see page 50), nickname of the former KGB's headquarters. To the right is the 19th-century Polytechnical Museum building (see page 58), while to the left is Russia's biggest toyshop, Detskiy Mir ('Children's World'). In a

sign of the times, most of the ground floor is occupied by a car showroom!
Metro: Lubyanka.

PLOSHCHAD REVOLYUTSII
(Revolution Square)
Remains of the 16th-century city walls back the square, a favourite site of communist demonstrations to this day. Shining behind the walls is the cupola of the Zaikonospasskiy Monastery (see page 72).

The ornate red brick City Duma (council) building, on the left as you leave the metro, was until recently the grandest of the USSR's many Lenin museums, exhibiting Lenin's works in well over 100 languages.
Metro: Ploshchad Revolyutsii.

PUSHKINSKAYA PLOSHCHAD
(Pushkin Square)
The elegant Strastnoy Monastery was torn down in 1937 to make room for this favourite Moscow meeting place at the intersection of Tverskaya Ulitsa and the Bulvar (see page 70).
Metro: Pushkinskaya, Tverskaya.

STARAYA PLOSHCHAD
(Old Square)
A thriving market place in the last century, Staraya Ploshchad was better known more recently as the home of the Communist Party Central Committee (building No 4), ideological epicentre of the Soviet Union. Some of the area's old

charm is captured in the 1694 Tserkov Vsyekh Svyatikh (Church of All Saints) at the far end of the square and the gloriously decorated Church of the Trinity on nearby Nikitnikov Pereulok (see page 73).
Metro: Kitay-gorod.

TAGANSKAYA PLOSHCHAD
(Taganka Square)

Much of the 19th-century anthill of artisans' dwellings, cheap hostels and taverns in this quarter was destroyed by Soviet town planners, leaving little more than the vast expanse of the square. However, it was celebrated under communism for the barely tolerated Taganka Theatre and its favourite son, Russia's Bob Dylan, Vladimir Vysotsky who died of drink in 1980.
Metro: Taganskaya.

Russia's national poet Alexander Pushkin presides over the square named after him

TEATRALNAYA PLOSHCHAD
(Theatre Square)

The Bolshoy (Big) Theatre, designed in 1825 by Osip Bove, is both an architectural and cultural Moscow landmark. Rivalled only by St Petersburg's Mariinskiy (formerly Kirov) Theatre, its stage has played host to attractions as diverse as the great singer Fedor Chaliapin and the 1922 founding ceremony of the Soviet Union. (See also pages 152–3.) It shares the square with the Children's Theatre and the Maliy (Small) Theatre, to its right and left respectively. A huge granite impression of Karl Marx looks across Teatralniy Proezd.

A ceramic frieze enlivens the outside of the luxuriously restored Metropol Hotel to Marx's right on Teatralniy Proezd. Constructed at the turn of the century, it's *style moderne* interior is well worth a look.
Metro: Teatralnaya, Okhotniy Ryad.

Tretyakovskaya Galereya
(Tretyakov Gallery)

*T*he Tretyakov Gallery boasts the largest collection of Russian art in the world (some 50,000 paintings in all). It was founded by the millionaire industrialist Pavel Tretyakov who presented his private collection to the city of Moscow in 1892. The original building was designed in the Russian revivalist style by Viktor Vasnetsov and completed in 1905.

The gallery was closed in 1985 for a comprehensive programme of restoration which is still incomplete. For the time being the bulk of the paintings are exhibited in the new wing. To make matters more confusing there is another picture gallery, the Novaya Tretyakovskaya Galereya (known familiarly as the Tretyakovka), devoted to art from the Soviet period. This is on a different site entirely.

The Tretyakov
The exhibition begins on the first floor of the new wing with a magnificent collection of icons. Icon painting, like Christianity itself, came to Russia via Byzantium. Most of the earliest icons are from Kiev, the cradle of Russian civilisation; the oldest, the austere *Virgin of Vladimir*, dates from the 11th century. The

The Last Judgement, a 15th-century icon of the Novgorod school

early schools of Kiev, Novgorod and Pskov paved the way for artists of the naturalistic Moscow school which flourished from the 14th to 17th centuries. There are masterpieces by the great trio of Moscow iconographers: Theophanes the Greek, Dionysius and Andrei Rublev, as well as the 17th-century master, Simon Ushakov.

The story of Russian art continues on the second floor with the European-trained painters of the Academy of Arts, founded by Catherine the Great in the 18th century. The works on show include portraits and landscapes by Dmitry Levitsky, Vladimir Borovikovskiy and Vasilu Tropinin.

In the 1870s a group of artists including Ivan Kramskoy, Vasily Perov and Fedor Vasilev, rebelled against the straitjacket of academicism and

A Small Yard in Moscow by Vasily Polenov

went in search of a new, national art. The subject matter of these artists, who became known as the *Peredvizhniki* (Wanderers) and went on to include Vasily Surikov, Vasily Polenov, Alexei Sarasov and the prolific Ilya Repin, ranges from portraits and vast historical canvases, through landscapes and religious paintings to vivid exposés of the horrors of war and the causes of social conflict (see also page 60). Within the space of a generation, the Wanderers had been overtaken by a new wave of artists including several future collaborators of Diaghilev's Ballets Russes: Valentin Serov, Alexander Benois and Konstantin Korovin.

In the 20th century Russian painters entered the vanguard of European art, with Mikhail Larionov, Natalya Goncharova and Kazimir Malevich. Their work is highly original but there is clear evidence too of the influence of the European Cubo-Futurist school. Many of these artists, including Vasily Kandinsky, were forced to leave Russia after the Revolution because of tightening ideological constraints which have only recently been relaxed.

The Tretyakovka

The New Tretyakov Gallery exhibits art of the communist era, as well as shows by contemporary Russian artists. Most of the Soviet art belongs to the Socialist Realist school which set out in the 1920s as an attempt to make art more accessible to the people, but which later degenerated into an ideological tool of the regime. What's on offer is a movable feast but some of the more original artists to look out for include Isaak Brodsky, Aleksandr Deyneka and Sergei Gerasimov. (See also page 39.)

Old site (Tretyakov): Lavrushinskiy Pereulok 12. Tel: 233 1050. Open: 10am–8pm (last admissions 7pm). Closed: Monday. Admission charge. Tours available in English. Metro: Tretyakovskaya.
New site (Tretyakovka): Krymskiy Val Ulitsa 10/14. Tel: 230 7788. Open: 10am–8pm. Closed: Monday. Admission charge. Tours available in English. Metro: Park Kultury.

ART AND PROPAGANDA

'You know what your art is?' Khrushchev asked the abstract painter Ernst Neizvestny at an exhibition in 1962. 'You go into a privy, climb through the hole and look up at what's above you when someone sits down ... That's what your art is, Comrade Neizvestny!' And Khrushchev was probably the most tolerant among the Soviet leaders.

Pravda savagely condemned 'bourgeois deviations' from the school of Socialist Realism, spelled out in the 1930s and later stridently reasserted by ideology chief A A Zhdanov (1896–1948). Dissenters like novelist Mikhail Bulgakov (1894–1941) and poet Anna Akhmatova (1888–1966) languished unpublished or in internal exile. Others, such as the artists Marc Chagall (1887–1986) and Vasily Kandinsky (1866–1944), left Russia never to return.

The composer Dmitri Shostakovich (1906–75) was only rehabilitated in 1956, having fallen foul of Zhdanov's command that the USSR should be 'the true protector of mankind's musical culture, a wall guarding human civilisation from bourgeois decay'.

Only works glorifying the Revolution and the common man were acceptable: the 1920s novel *Cement*, relating the heroic exploits of construction labourers, was held aloft as an example; the Moscow metro system was celebrated in a ceremonial march; and a theatre shaped like a tractor was built in Rostov-on-Don.

At the outbreak of revolution,

Left: mural in
Moscow
Above and right:
politics in posters

Russia's artists
had enjoyed a
brief but explosive
period of avant-
garde
experimentation.
The proto-punk
verses of Vladimir
Mayakovsky
(1893–1930)
spearheaded the Futurist movement.
Kasimir Malevich (1878–1935) fronted
the Suprematist school of design, while

Vladimir Tatlin
(1885–1953) and the
Constructivists
declared
'uncompromising war'
on Diaghilev's 'art for
art's sake'.

The Socialist-
Realist movement
that followed derived
its authority from
Lenin's favourite
radical, Nikolai
Chernyshevsky
(1828–89). 'Reality is more beautiful than
its representation in art' was his slogan –
a slogan slowly turned on its head by
idealised portraits of happy workers.

Tverskaya Ulitsa and Patriarshiy Prud

Named after the market town of Tver 150km north of Moscow, Tverskaya Ulitsa's broad expanse begins the long highway to St Petersburg. It was reconstructed as Gorky Street in the 1930s to Stalin's grandiose taste. The up-market shops demonstrate the new-found wealth of many Muscovites; the contrastingly peaceful environs are the focus of much of the capital's literary history. *Allow 2½ hours.*

Begin at Mayakovskaya metro station.

1 TRIUMFALNAYA PLOSHCHAD
'Comrades, to the barricades!... Streets are our brushes, squares are our palettes!' Thus exhorted the poet Vladimir Mayakovsky, the laureate of Soviet communism, whose statue dominates the square (which also used to bear his name). Behind him stands the resolutely Stalinist Peking Hotel while to his right are Kontsertniy Zal im P I Tchaikovskovo (Tchaikovsky Concert Hall) and Teatr Satiry (Theatre of Satire).

Bear down Tverskaya Ulitsa towards the Kremlin.

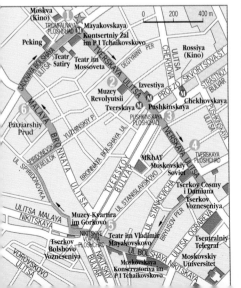

2 MUZEY REVOLYUTSII
(Museum of the Revolution)
The exhibits here offer a balanced view of Russia's unsettled politics to the present day. The crumpled trolleybus in the forecourt came abreast of a tank during the abortive 1991 coup. (See page 57.)

3 PUSHKINSKAYA PLOSHCHAD
In summer amorous couples and drunks compete for benches in the shade around the statue of Russia's national poet, Alexander Pushkin, to whom the square is dedicated. For centuries a favourite meeting place, it is now the site of the

Patriarch's Ponds, a
peaceful refuge

world's largest
McDonald's
restaurant. A
ferment of poets,
politics and black
market traders in
the late 1980s, it
now harbours
pickpockets rather
than *agents
provocateurs*.
*Continue down the
left of the street*

4 INNER TVERSKAYA ULITSA

Passing the waxworks museum at No 14
(see page 156), the faded glory of the
adjoining Yeliseev's food store is worth a
look before reaching Tverskaya
Ploshchad where Moscow's founder,
Yuri Dolgorukiy, faces the city council
building. A world-weary Lenin sits in
isolation to his rear, oblivious of the
reconstruction to his left of 18th-century
Tserkov Cosmy i Damiana (SS Cosma
and Damian Church), till recently the
Culture Ministry printing works.

The façades of Nos 9 and 11 across
the road are built of granite earmarked
by the Germans for a victory monument
following the expected fall of Moscow.
Through the arch gleams the cupola of
the delicate Tserkov Vozneseniya
(Church of the Ascension), built in 1629.
*Continue along Bryusov Pereulok to Ulitsa
Bolshaya Nikitskaya and out of the centre.*

5 LITERARY MOSCOW

The TASS news agency stands at the
corner of Ulitsa Bolshaya Nikitskaya and
the Bulvar. Author Maxim Gorky is
remembered in the art nouveau house-
museum (Muzey-Kvartira im Gorkovo)
at nearby Ulitsa Malaya Nikitskaya 6/2
(see page 59). Next comes the house
(under reconstruction) of poet Alexander
Blok; opposite lived the officially
approved writer Alexei Tolstoy, a distant
relative of *the* Tolstoy.
*Turn right on Ulitsa Spiridonovka then
right along Spiridonevski Pereulok, then left
on to Malaya Bronnaya Ulitsa.*

6 BULGAKOV'S MOSCOW

When the Devil comes to torment
Moscow in Mikhail Bulgakov's
masterpiece *The Master and Margarita*,
he makes his first appearance at the
tranquil Patriarshiy Prud (Patriarch's
Ponds). The novel was suppressed by
Stalin and was not published until 1966.
Its author died blind and penniless in
1940. Much of the action is set around
the corner in apartment 50, Sadovaya
Bolshaya Ulitsa 10, where Bulgakov lived
in the early 1920s. The graffiti festooning
the staircase bear witness to the cult-like
following he enjoys to this day.
*Turn right on to Sadovaya Bolshaya Ulitsa
to return to Mayakovskaya.*

Kitay Gorod

The financial heart of Moscow till the Revolution, Kitay Gorod is one of the longest inhabited parts of the capital and largely escaped the brutal Soviet town planning of the 1930s. Impregnable battlements and proximity to the Kremlin attracted artisans' guilds in the Middle Ages, while the concentration of wealth and strict monastic orders played their part in establishing Russia's first centre of learning. *Allow 1½ hours.*

Start at metro Lubyanka and head down Teatralniy Proezd to the Nikolskiy Gates.

1 NIKOLSKIY VOROTA (Nikolskiy Gates)

This is the last remaining of seven former gateways in the mighty walls around Kitay Gorod. The name of the stronghold probably derives from the wooden laths (*kiti*) built into the walls for strength.

Head through the arch and turn right along Nikolskaya Ulitsa. The Slavyanskiy Bazaar restaurant at No 7 was a favourite haunt of Russian literati, including the writer Chekhov, the theatre director Stanislavsky and the composers Rimsky-Korsakov and Tchaikovsky.

2 THE RUSSIAN RENAISSANCE

An elaborate stucco façade decorates the turquoise building at No 15, erected in Russian Gothic style on the site of the former Synodal Printing House. Here in 1564 Ivan Fedorov set the type of *The Acts of the Apostles*, Russia's first book. Further down the street in the courtyard of No 9 is another crucible of the Russian Renaissance, the 17th-century Zaikonospasskiy Monastery. The greenish building at the back of the yard was the Slavic-Greek-Latin Academy, Russia's first university. The recently reopened Spasskiy Sobor (Spasskiy Cathedral), once one of the greatest examples of Russian baroque

architecture, suffered use as a dormitory for metro engineers and a dog-lovers' club under the Soviets.
Retrace your steps and turn right down Bogoyavlenskiy Pereulok.

3 FINANCIAL MOSCOW
Facing you at the end of the street is the classical portico of the Stock Exchange (*birzha*) building, now the Chamber of Commerce (Torgovaya Palata). Beside it on Ulitsa Ilinka and Rybniy Pereulok stands what was once the mercantile heart of Russia, the Old Merchants' Chambers or 'Gostiniy Dvor', marketplace of traders from all over the empire.

Heading along Ulitsa Ilinka, note the imposing black façade of the Ministry of Finance at No 9. No 27 is the grandiose premises of the Northern Insurance Society, now home to Russia's Constitutional Court.
Turn right along Staraya Ploshchad (see page 64), then right into Nikitnikov Pereulok before turning right down Ipatevskiy Pereulok.

4 TSERKOV TROITSY V NIKITNIKAKH (Church of the Trinity in Nikitnikakhi)
The delicate red and white spade gables contribute to the beauty of one of Moscow's most celebrated churches, completed in 1653. The frescos and iconostasis are largely the work of the master Simon Ushakov.
Turn right on to Ulitsa Varvarka.

5 ULITSA VARVARKA
The hulking Rossiya Hotel (1967) dominates this street of glorious little churches which miraculously escaped the demolition of a whole district prior to the hotel's construction. At No 12 rise the

The imposing bulk of Moscow's Chamber of Commerce building on Ulitsa Ilinka

five indigo cupolas studded with gold stars of the 17th-century Tserkov Giorgiya (Church of St George), now a shop selling folk arts and crafts. Next door is the Romanov House, built by Mikhail Romanov's grandfather (see page 56).

The simple Tserkov Maksima Blazhennovo (Church of St Maxim the Blessed) stands at No 6, while the Rossiya's nightclub faces the 16th-century Angliyskoe Podvore (English Residence), donated by Ivan the Terrible to members of the London Muscovy Company. The street comes to an end with the pastel exterior of the classical Tserkov Velikomuchenitsy Varvary (Church of St Barbara).

The Arbat

Dirty-kneed children and frock-coated merchants ... the last decades of a doomed aristocracy ... underground printing presses and impoverished artists ... this is the soul of the Arbat quarter of the city that still filters through today's pedestrian mall and souvenir shops. The grimy courtyards and twisting back streets readily conjure up scenes of working-class life at the inception of the Revolution, while the time-worn mansions of Ulitsa Prechistenka speak of an age never to return. *Allow 2½ hours.*

Start at metro Arbatskaya. Take a look at the vast Ministry of Defence (Ministervo Oboroniy) building behind you before crossing the road to Ulitsa Arbat.

1 ULITSA ARBAT

Alive with street musicians, beggars, snappily-dressed *mafiosi* and long-haired youth, the Arbat retains something of the bohemian atmosphere of days gone by. The region around the street played host at various times to such luminaries as writers Pushkin, Lermontov, Tolstoy, Gogol and Bulgakov and composers Scriabin and Rachmaninov.

The street was also a hotbed of political dissent – the basement of No 9 housed one of the country's largest anti-tsarist printing presses.

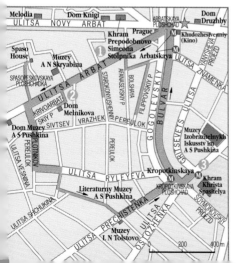

Once the main route to Russia's western lands, the Arbat was the road to Stalin's dacha in the 1930s, patrolled by a legion of secret police for whom the luxurious Praga restaurant (on the right-hand corner) was converted into a dining hall. The concentration of intelligentsia made the area a prime target of Stalin's terror, as recorded in Anatoly Rybakov's novel *Children of the Arbat* – hugely popular during the *glasnost* era. The author lived at No 51. *Make a detour left down Bolshaya Afanasevskiy Pereulok, immediately left again and then right on to Filippovskiy Pereulok.*

A jazz band contributing to the atmosphere of Ulitsa Arbat, one of Moscow's liveliest areas

2 SIDE STREETS

As you make your way along the Arbat, duck into as many of the courtyards and side streets as you can: each has its own fascination. Starokonyushenniy Pereulok 36, where Scriabin used to give concerts, is a wonderful example of the Russian carved *izba* (wooden cottage). Further along, Krivoarbatskiy Pereulok 10 was the home of the modernist architect Konstantin Melnikov, dubbed 'the Russian Le Corbusier', whose genius was ultimately snuffed out by Stalin – for 40 years, until his death in 1974, not one of Melnikov's projects was realised. To the right up Spasopeskovskiy Pereulok is the residence of US Ambassadors to Russia, Spaso House, built in 1914 for the financier Nikolai Vtorov (later murdered by a Red Army guard). Return to Ulitsa Arbat then go down Plotnikov Pereulok.

Wander south through the embassies of one of the city's most fashionable residential districts until you come to Ulitsa Prechistenka, the aristocratic stronghold of old Moscow. No 12 is now Literaturniy Muzey A S Pushkina, a museum devoted to the poet Pushkin, while No 11, Muzey L N Tolstovo, is dedicated to Tolstoy (see page 59).

3 KHRAM KHRISTA SPASITELYA

Until 1934, this was the site of the vast Cathedral of Christ the Saviour whose dome dominated the city skyline. It was blown up to make way for what was to have been the world's largest building, Stalin's Palace of Soviets. Inexplicably, the foundations continuously flooded, and Khrushchev abandoned the project, digging out a swimming pool (Basseyn Moskva) instead. The unsanitary state of the pool forced city authorities to close it in 1993, and work is currently underway on the cathedral's reconstruction. *Muzey Izobrazitelnykh Iskusstv im A S Pushkina (Pushkin Fine Arts Museum) is at Ulitsa Volkhonka 12 (see page 38). Take Gogolevskiy Bulvar to metro Arbatskaya.*

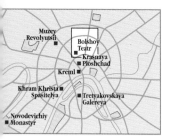

Kuznetskiy Most and the Neglinnaya

A little of the 19th-century exclusivity of Kuznetskiy Most is being reborn in brightly-lit shop windows, while the back streets giving on to the Bulvar reach deep into Moscow's medieval past. *Allow 1½ hours, excluding visits to the steam baths and circus.*

Head straight for Kuznetskiy Most from the metro station of the same name.

1 THE NEGLINNAYA RIVER

Kuznetskiy Most – Smiths' Bridge – is named after the metalworkers in the cannon foundry established on the left bank of the Neglinnaya river by Ivan the Terrible. Though the bridge was dismantled when the river was enclosed underground, its name lived on in the city's centre of finance and fashion. The jeweller Fabergé displayed his marvels in today's 'Rifle' clothing shop, No 21/5 was the headquarters of the first Russian Insurance Society, while around the corner at Neglinnaya Ulitsa 12 stands the Central Bank of the Russian Federation.

Continue along Neglinnaya Ulitsa, then turn right into Neglinnaya Pereulok.

2 SANDUNOVSKIYE BANYI (Sandunovskiy Baths)

Much loved by Moscow's literati – the author Chekhov had a private room overlooking No 2 – the historic steam baths at Neglinnaya Pereulok 14 are worth a look. The interior, with its carved oak cubicles, stained glass and elegant light fittings dating from the early 19th century, breathes faded grandeur. (For details on Russian 'banya' procedures, see page 158.)

Turn left at the end of Neglinnaya Pereulok on to Ulitsa Rozhdestvenka.

3 TO STRETENSKIY MONASTYR

The 18th-century country house to the left with the prettily tiled façade is Moscow's Architectural Institute and Tserkov Nikolaya v Zvonaryakh (Church of St Nicholas in Zvonaryakh) next door, named after the Kremlin bellringers who lived near by, houses the institute's drawing school.

Turning down Bolshoy Kiselny Pereulok and left on to Ulitsa Lubyanka Bolshaya, you come to the remains of the Stretenskiy Monastery, founded in 1395. Built in honour of the miraculous icon which came to Tamerlane in a dream and dissuaded him from attacking Moscow, the cathedral and its glorious frescos are now under restoration following years of abuse as a club for the KGB.

4 ROZHDESTVENSKIY BULVAR AND MONASTYR

The most elegant of the capital's boulevards begins with the tiny chapel of Our Lady Most Holy, attached to a church occupied by a derelict naval museum. Opposite on Stretenskiy Bulvar a statue to Lenin's wife, Nadezhda Krupskaya, stands in place of the Stretenskiy Gates – pulled down by Stalin in the 1930s.

The far left corner of Rozhdestvenskiy Bulvar is the site of an ancient convent, constructed in 1386 on the upper banks of the Neglinnaya river. Although the convent was closed soon after the Revolution, two old nuns, Varvara and Viktorina, continued to live there until the former was strangled by an icon-smuggler in 1978. The convent has recently reopened.

Enjoy the view over the rooftops from the end of the boulevard and walk down to the square.

5 TRUBNAYA PLOSHCHAD AND TSVETNOY BULVAR

Trubnaya Ploshchad used to be the site of a bustling livestock market. On Annunciation Day (25 March), Muscovites traditionally bought birds and released them into the air – profitable business for the traders who trained them to return for subsequent resale. Neighbouring Tsvetnoy Bulvar was the city's main flower market but is now loved for the Tsirq (State Circus – see page 157) on the left.

Tsvetnoy Bulvar metro station is just beyond the circus.

Rooftop detail of the old Rozhdestvenskiy convent, open again after Soviet closure

Zamoskvoreche

Translating as 'Beyond the Moscow River', this area was the city's wild frontier in the Middle Ages, a densely forested region manned by isolated Cossack outposts on the main highway to the settlements of the dreaded Tartar Khans. Subsequently, Moscow's gentry chose Zamoskvoreche for their city estates, and the wealth of classical mansions and graceful churches ideally complements a visit to the main attraction, the Tretyakov Gallery. *Allow 2 hours, excluding the Tretyakov Gallery.*

Start from Oktyabrskaya metro.

1 KALUZHSKAYA PLOSHCHAD (formerly October Square)

A colossal statue of Lenin dominates this square, a favourite site for communist demonstrations. Moving down Ulitsa

Bolshaya Yakimanka (to Lenin's right), note the fanciful French Embassy, built at the turn of the century in a pastiche Old Russian style. Opposite rise the chequered cupolas of Tserkov Muchenika Ioanna Voyna (Church of St John the Warrior), a breathtaking example of early 18th-century religious architecture.
Turn right down Khvostov Pereulok to Ulitsa Polyanka Bolshaya.

2 ULITSA POLYANKA BOLSHAYA

Facing you as you join Ulitsa Polyanka Bolshaya is the 1695 Church of the Dormition. Down the street at No 29a is the attractive Tserkov Grigoriya (Church of St Gregory), a wonderful multi-coloured confection dating from the 17th century.
Retrace your steps 50m and turn down peaceful Staromonetniy Pereulok, taking the second right into Bolshoy Tolmachevskiy Pereulok.

3 AROUND THE TRETYAKOVSKAYA

On the right of the street at No 3 stands one of Moscow's finest classical mansions, built in 1770 for the fantastically wealthy Siberian mining magnate Demidov. On the left is the Church of St Nicholas, now part of the Tretyakov Gallery (see pages 66–7).
Walk ahead to Bolshaya Ordynka Ulitsa and head right to No 34.

4 MARFO-MARIANSKIY OBITEL (Convent of SS Martha and Mary)

Assisted by the greatest contemporary artists, Grand Duchess Yelizaveta Fedorovna founded this convent in 1908 after her husband Sergei, the governor of Moscow, was blown up by a revolutionary's bomb. The Church of the Virgin's Veil was built in the ancient Novgorod style by A V Shchusev, who went on to design Lenin's mausoleum. The grand duchess's cells house the laundry of a hospital now occupying the grounds. She herself was executed with the rest of the royal family in 1918.
Return towards the centre along Bolshaya Ordynka Ulitsa.

5 BOLSHAYA ORDYNKA ULITSA

In the 14th century, this was the chief road along which the Tartar horde invaded Moscow demanding tribute and slaves. The churches and pre-revolutionary estates make for a rare tranquillity. Note especially the baroque masterpiece Tserkov Klimenta (Church of St Clement, to the right down Klimentovskiy Pereulok) and Tserkov

The fine early 18th-century Church of St John the Warrior

Vsyekh Skorbyashikh Radosty (Church of the Joy of All who Sorrow), funded in 1834 by the merchant Dolgov who lived in the mansion opposite.
Cut down Chernigovskiy Pereulok.

6 TO THE KREMLIN

On the right you come to the small stone Tserkov Chernigovskikh Chudddtvortsev (Church of the Chernigov Miracle Workers), after which the lane is named, and to the left the ensemble of Tserkov Ioana (Church of St John). Turning left on to well-preserved Pyatnitskaya Ulitsa, note on the right-hand corner the restored headquarters of the original Smirnoff vodka company – the words read 'Supplier to his Imperial Majesty, Pyotr Arsenyevich Smirnov'. A battle is now raging between the original Smirnovs and the US-owned distillers over lucrative rights to the family name.
Cross the bridge to continue towards the Kremlin.

Excursions from Moscow

ABRAMTSEVO

This tranquil country estate, set among woods and ponds, is best known as the retreat of a group of artists, 'The Wanderers' (see page 60). The railway magnate Savva Mamontov bought the house and grounds in 1870; under his patronage painters such as Ilya Repin, Mikhail Vrubel and Viktor Vasnetsov produced some of their finest work.

Much is now in the Russian Museum in St Petersburg (see page 114), but copies of the group's paintings hang in the main estate building, the peaceful landscapes and delicate portraits of Mamontov's daughters capturing the intimacy of the setting. Pen and ink sketches show costumes from the family plays put on in the evenings. The great opera singer Fedor Chaliapin was one of the many visiting celebrities who signed the tablecloth on display.

Abramtsevo, a rural retreat for artists at odds with the establishment

The Church of Our Saviour among the trees is the result of collaboration by the artists: Vasily Polenov designed the beautiful iconostasis while the icon of the Saviour is the work of Repin. Mamontov is buried in the adjoining chapel.
Reach by elektrichka *(80 minutes) from Yaroslavskiy Vokzal, or drive down Yaroslavskoye Shosse towards Sergiev Posad until signpost to Abramtsevo. Tel: 8 254 32470. Open: Wednesday to Sunday 10am–5pm. Closed: last Thursday of the month. Admission charge.*

BORODINO

Over 100,000 troops died in one day in 1812 on Russia's most famous battlefield, now a vast museum-reserve littered with memorials to the bitter end of Napoleon's plans to capture Moscow. A museum tells the story of General Bagration and Marshal Kutuzov who led the Russian effort, with Bagration's grave a short walk to the east. Mass graves and trenches remain elsewhere about the site,

What would Lenin have thought of this capitalistic enterprise at his country estate, Leninskie Gorki?

testament to the 1941 bitter engagement at Borodino during World War II.

A dramatic re-enactment of the Napoleonic battle, complete with bayonet charges and cavalry, takes place yearly on the weekend nearest 7 September (details from museum).

Borodino is 124km from Moscow. Take elektrichka from Belorusskiy Vokzal and walk 3km from Borodino station to museum. By car, take Minskoye Shosse to Mozhaisk; Borodino village is 12km west. Tel: 8 238 51057. Open 10am–6pm. Closed: Monday. Admission charge.

LENINSKIE GORKI

In the heyday of Soviet power, half a million visitors a year paid homage at the estate where Lenin died, aged 53, in January 1924 after a series of strokes. Here he spelled out his 'final testament' with its famous warning: 'Comrade Stalin has concentrated unlimited authority in his hands and I am not sure whether he will always be capable of using that authority with sufficient caution.'

Clocks in the estate are stopped at 5.50, the time of his death, and though the premises are falling into disrepair, some curios remain such as Lenin's personal Rolls-Royce, adapted for Russia with skis and a half-track rear drive.

Leninskie Gorki is 35km south of Moscow. Take elektrichka from Paveletskiy Vokzal then bus 27 or 28. By car take Kashirskoye Shosse. Tel: 548 9309. Open: 10am–6pm. Closed: Tuesday. Admission charge.

MARFINO

This peaceful village north of Moscow harbours the remains of an estate belonging to Peter the Great's tutor, Prince Golitsyn. Built in the early 18th century, it was destroyed by Napoleon's forces during the advance on Moscow before being partially rebuilt with baroque flourishes. The estate has been spoilt by conversion into a Soviet workers' pension, but the picturesque lakeside setting makes for a superior summer picnic spot.

Take elektrichka from Savyolovskiy Vokzal to Katuar station (40 minutes), then catch bus 37 to estate gates. By car, drive down Dmitrovskoye Shosse until Marfino signpost.

St Sergius Trinity
Monastery, Sergiev
Posad: the Refectory

the turn of the century, from the fur coat hanging in the hallway to the spartan furnishings of his bedroom and the separate kitchen and scullery where Chekhov taught the cook to read in the mornings. The cosy middle-class atmosphere, worlds apart from urban Moscow, is a rare reminder of a lifestyle otherwise found only in the pages of Chekhov's own stories.

Melikhovo is 60km south of Moscow. Take elektrichka *from Kurskiy Vokzal to Chekhov, then bus 25. By car, drive down Varshavskoye Shosse towards Tula till sign for Melikhovo. Chekhov estate, tel: 8 272 23610. Open: Wednesday to Sunday 10am–4pm. Closed: last Friday of month.*

MELIKHOVO

Anton Chekhov (1860–1904) wrote his ground-breaking play *The Seagull* and many of his short stories at his country estate here. The modest estate is a little barren in winter but its wild gardens are enchanting in summer or when the surrounding meadows burst with bluebells in early spring.

The buildings have been carefully preserved to capture the writer's life at

MONINO

A rare chance to see the hardware which kept NATO on its toes and with which General Secretary Khrushchev promised to bury the west is on offer at this working airbase not far from Moscow. One field is set aside to display the key elements of Soviet airpower, known in the west by codenames such as 'Flogger', 'Bear' and 'Sabre'. The exhibition includes the mighty Bison bomber, capable of flying to Washington, dropping its payload and returning to Moscow, and the civilian Tupoleyev 144 'Concordski' which never saw regular service.

For security clearance, tours have to be booked well ahead.

Reach Monino town by elektrichka *from Yaroslavskiy Vokzal (the airbase north entrance is a short walk from the station) or by car along Shosse Entuziastov. Muzey Istorii Aviatsii (Monino Airforce Museum), tel: 526 3327, 584 2180. Visits by prior arrangement only. Admission charge.*

PEREDELKINO

This little village is best known as the Soviet Union's writers' colony where the politically correct were rewarded with luxurious country retreats. Its most famous resident was author and poet Boris Pasternak (1890–1960). He lived in virtual exile here after being forced in 1957 to decline the Nobel Prize for his most famous work, *Dr Zhivago*, whose anti-revolutionary slant and worldwide success infuriated the Kremlin.

Pasternak's house is now a museum and his nearby grave is still smothered with bouquets from a grateful and respectful nation. Both are best located with the help of a friendly local.

Peredelkino is 25km west of Moscow. Reach by elektrichka *from Kievskaya Vokzal, or by road via Kutuzovskiy Prospekt and Minskoye Shosse until left turn at the 21km post. Pasternak's house open: Thursday and Sunday 10am–4pm. Admission charge.*

SERGIEV POSAD

Formerly known as Zagorsk, this town is focused around one of Orthodox Russia's key sites, the magnificent Troitse-Sergievskaya Lavra (St Sergius Trinity Monastery). Remarkable for its wealth of history and church architecture, the monastery was the home of the Patriarch under Soviet rule and remains an epicentre of Russia's Orthodox revival. Dress should be modest; tourists now take a definite second place to pilgrims and seminary students.

The monastery was founded in the 14th century by Russia's patron saint, Sergius of Radonezh, who was instrumental in organising resistance to the Tartar occupation of Muscovy. Its eerie Trinity Cathedral, adorned with priceless icons by the great Andrei Rublev, holds a permanent lamplit service to the saint.

The atmosphere in winter is unforgettable, from the dusting of snow on the azure and gold domes of the Cathedral of the Assumption, to the pungent incense, rich decoration and bass chants within.

Sergiev Posad is 75km north of Moscow. Reached by elektrichka *from Yaroslavskiy Vokzal (1½ hours) or by car via Yaroslavskoye Shosse. Monastery open: 10am–5pm. Closed: Monday and weekends. Admission charge.*

Golden domes of Trinity Cathedral, Sergiev Posad, where St Sergius lies buried

Zolotoe Koltso

Zolotoe Koltso (the Golden Ring) is the name of a series of medieval towns at the very heart of Russian history. Following the decline of the great Kievan state, each became a separate principality and trading centre before the Tartar invasions and eventual absorption by Muscovy.

The main towns remain some of the best preserved and most memorable destinations of any trip to Russia – the impregnable kremlins, exquisite churches and congested markets evoke the essence of the country's feudal past. Many tours to Moscow include one or more in their itinerary. None of the towns described below (except perhaps Zvenigorod) makes for a sensible day trip. Good hotel accommodation is available, often inside the monasteries. Detailed handbooks to the region are freely available in Moscow.

The wooden Preobrazhenskaya church, Suzdal, one of many architectural treasures here

ROSTOV VELIKI

'Rostov the Great' was founded on the shores of Ozero Nero (Lake Nero) as early as the 9th century and is famed for its outstanding fortress, or kremlin, built in the late 1600s. Within its walls are several gloriously decorated churches; outside, the Uspenskaya Tserkov (Church of the Assumption) steals the scene while a number of ancient monasteries are within easy reach of the town centre.

SUZDAL

Suzdal is the true gem of the Golden Ring, a sleepy rural town 220km from Moscow, packed with picturesque churches and rickety wooden cottages about the slow-moving Kamenka river. At its zenith, Suzdal boasted over 70 churches and monasteries, many donated by merchants grown rich on the city's fertile land. Even those daunted by the prospect of more onion domes and icons will be delighted by perhaps Russia's most beautiful tourist attraction.

VLADIMIR

Once Russia's capital, the ancient city of Vladimir is now a grubby textile and defence industry centre 180km east of Moscow.

Bird's-eye view of Yaroslavl on the Volga river. Trade brought wealth in the 13th and 16th centuries

Today the city is racked by the modern evils of unemployment and pollution, but its glorious past as the headquarters of Russia's medieval strongman Yuri Dolgorukiy is still reflected in a number of architectural masterpieces. The 1158 Uspenskiy Sobor (Cathedral of the Assumption) on the heights above the river was the model for its namesake in the Moscow Kremlin and housed the revered Vladimir Mother of God icon, now displayed in the Tretyakov Gallery (see pages 66–7).

YAROSLAVL

Founded as a trading post on the Volga river, Yaroslavl is the largest of the Golden Ring cities. Like its neighbours, it was ransacked by the Tartars but emerged as a flourishing princedom hosting English and Dutch traders travelling to Moscow from Archangelsk on the White Sea. Fortified monasteries and the lavish 17th-century Tserkov Ioana Zlatousta (Church of St John Chrysostom) recall its former days of mercantile splendour.

ZVENIGOROD

The hilltop city of Zvenigorod was founded at the end of the 13th century in what is known as the 'Russian Switzerland', a lovely landscape at its best as the leaves turn with the onset of winter.

On the road heading out of town, note the remains of the old city kremlin, climbing from the Moskva river. A footpath leads to the graceful Uspenskaya Tserkov (Church of the Assumption, 1396) on top of the hill. A little further up the road lies the magnificent white-stone Savvino-Strozhevskiy monastery. It was closed down in 1919, but restoration is fast resurrecting the gatehouse church and the monastery cathedral. Andrei Rublev, greatest of Russia's icon masters, decorated the cathedral and in 1918 three of his original icons were discovered in a wood shed on the hilltop. They are now on view in Moscow's Tretyakov Gallery. *Zvenigorod is 90 minutes by elektrichka from Belorusskiy Vokzal or one hour by car along Uspenskoye Shosse. Monastery open: 10am–5pm. Closed: Monday. Admission charge.*

COUNTRY LIFE

A short ride on a suburban train leaves behind the city's emerging sophistication and takes the traveller back in time to an entirely different world – the Russian countryside.

Vast expanses of farmland, isolated cottages huddled under the severe northern sky, and headscarved women sitting beneath brightly-decorated window frames watching strangers with a wary eye: it's a picture that changes little the length and breadth of Russia.

The almost idyllic scenes often conceal a life of extreme hardship. The stoicism of the Russian *muzhik* – peasant – is legendary, facing changes in politics and the weather with the same dour patience. The older among them vividly remember the terror and famines of one of Stalin's most senseless policies, collectivisation, from which country life has scarcely begun to recover.

Historians reckon that 14 million were killed in the 1930s, either by starvation,

Far left: haymaking on Yelagin Island, St Petersburg. Left and below: the unchanging face of peasant life, most Russians' roots

firing squad or in exile, as a result of the forcible destruction of private farming to create gigantic collective farms and communist 'agrotowns'. Wealthy peasants, dubbed *kulaki* or 'tight fists', were singled out for special treatment: 'We must smash the kulaks, eliminate them as a class,' Stalin ordered.

Those who resisted were sent to labour camps in Siberia or shot in their villages. Stealing one ear of corn was classified as robbing the state and punishable by up to 10 years' imprisonment. One boy, Pavlik Morozov,

who denounced his father for hoarding grain, was held aloft as an example to Soviet children. Streets are still named after him in Moscow.

For all its suffering, the village community is still at the heart of the Russian nation. Before the Revolution, 90 per cent of the population lived in the country. Most of today's city-dwellers are only a generation or two removed from the fields – perhaps accounting for the popular saying that Moscow is 'just one big village'.

Sankt Peterburg
(St Petersburg)

St Petersburg is one of the world's most beautiful – and paradoxical – of cities. Its lasting impression is one of melancholy elegance, with its eerie 'white nights' of June and the frosty winter sun glancing off the stiletto spire of SS Peter and Paul Cathedral. The juxtaposition of its northerly isolation and classical west European architecture make it a living metaphor of the geographical schizophrenia lying behind the centuries-old struggle for Russia's soul between 'westernisers' and 'slavophiles' – a struggle still played out in the political rhetoric and armed confrontation of today.

A window on to Europe

St Petersburg was built on the River Neva at the point where it joins the Gulf of Finland. Peter the Great, convinced that rapid westernisation was essential to Russia's becoming a European power, cut the first turf in 1703. Initially a desolate military outpost, the city was to become Peter's 'window on to Europe, through which western commerce and culture would be shipped into Russia.'

Building the city demanded a superhuman effort: nobles were ordered to leave Moscow and resettle, thousands of serfs perished, building in stone was forbidden elsewhere, and every visitor had to pay a tax of several large rocks.

The splendour of Imperial Russia is celebrated in St Petersburg's architecture – not least that of the Winter Palace

Canalscape, with St Nicholas Cathedral

ST PETERSBURG TOWN PLAN

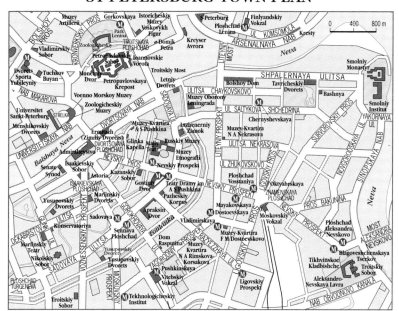

whose lavish state rooms ironically witnessed in 1917 the birth of Russia's new order, with the eviction by the Red Guards of the last exhausted members of the Provisional Government.

The politics of a name
During World War I, the city's name was changed to the less Germanic 'Petrograd'. In 1924 the Bolsheviks renamed it 'Leningrad'. The name 'St Petersburg' was readopted by referendum in 1991 when the flush of anti-Soviet enthusiasm was at its most passionate, but many of its 5 million inhabitants continue to call the city Leningrad.

BRIDGE OPENING TIMES

When travelling at night, keep in mind the times when bridges over the Neva are opened to let shipping through. If you get stuck, your only hope is to bargain with a boatman to ferry you across.

Dvortsovy Most 1.55–3.05am; 3.15–4.45am

Nikolaevskiy Most 1.55–2.55am; 3.15–4.50am

Troitskiy Most 2–4.40am

Tuchkov Most 2–3.10am; 3.40–4.40am

Bolshoy Krestovskiy Most 2.05–2.35am; 4.45–5.20am

Liteyniy Most 2.10–4.40am

Sampsonievskiy Most 2.10–2.25am; 3.20–4.45am

Kamennoostrovskiy Most 2.15–3am; 4.05–4.50am

Birzhevoy Most 2.25–3.30am; 3.40–4.40am

Most Aleksandra Nevskovo 2.35–4.50am.

ALEKSANDRO-NEVSKIY LAVRA (Alexander Nevsky Monastery)

The monastery was founded by Peter the Great, supposedly on the site of Prince Alexander Nevsky's 1240 victory over the Swedes. Today, the peeling paintwork of official neglect, cripples lining the drive and crows fluttering above the graveyards combine to leave a haunting impression.

Blagoveshchenskaya Tserkov (Cathedral of the Annunciation)

Designed by Peter's chief builder Domenico Trezzini, this church once served as the Romanovs' necropolis and still contains the tomb of Russia's greatest military mind, General Suvorov (1730–1800). Sadly, it houses a bankrupt museum of revolutionary statues which, outpaced by events, is 'closed for repairs'. The adjoining red-and-white monastery buildings, fine examples of Petrine architecture, are occupied by the city blood donation centre and likewise closed.

Cemeteries

A gateway in the right-hand wall of the drive leads to the Tikhvinskoe Kladbishche (Tikhvin Cemetery), containing the graves of some of Russia's greatest artists, including writer Dostoevsky and composers Mussorgsky and Rimsky-Korsakov. In the far right corner, a harrowing bust captures the exhausted soul of Tchaikovsky who committed suicide in 1893.

Opposite, the Lazarus cemetery is chiefly the resting place of aristocracy but also contains the graves of the scholar Lomonosov, Pushkin's wife Natalia Goncharova and many of the city's architects.

Troitskiy Sobor (Cathedral of the Trinity)

Catherine the Great's taste for classicism created a headache for the architect Ivan Starov, charged with blending Orthodox traditions and European architecture. Yet he succeeded – the vast interior (1790), for all its ornamentation, retains a peculiarly Orthodox intimacy. The remains of Alexander Nevsky, canonised by the church, lie in a silver sarcophagus to the right of the iconostasis. (As this is a working church, women should cover their heads.)

Ploshchad Aleksandra Nevskovo. Tel: 274 0409. Monastery open: 10.30am–6.30pm. Closed: Thursday. Tikhvin Cemetery open to 8pm; Lazarus to 5.45pm. Admission charge. Metro: Ploshchad Aleksandra Nevskovo.

AVRORA (Cruiser *Aurora*)

A blank shot from the bow cannon of this tiny warship gave the signal for Red Guards to take the Winter Palace in October 1917 (see pages 12–13), sealing the fate of the Provisional Government and securing the *Aurora* an almost legendary status in Soviet revolutionary hagiography.

Rimsky-Korsakov's grave in the Tikhvin Cemetery

The cruiser *Aurora*. A shot from here signalled the Revolution

One shot that shook the world

Docked for a routine refit in wartime Petrograd, the crew of the *Aurora* were among the first to switch allegiance to Lenin, who promised a swift end to an unpopular World War I. On the night of 24–25 October, they slipped anchor and moored downstream, 'threatening with true gunboat diplomacy' the foundering Provisional Government led by Alexander Kerensky across the river in the Winter Palace.

At 9.40pm, Seaman Yevdokim Ognev blasted the blank shot signalling the Bolsheviks' final thrust for power. The Provisional Government was soon overcome, bringing to a premature close Russia's short-lived experiment with democracy. Aboard the ship, Lenin broadcast his jubilant victory address to the people from the radio room.

Floating museum

Today you are free to wander around the immaculately preserved ship, inspect the cannon and take a look at the radio room. A mock-up of sailing conditions – the ship's menu records that Baltic Fleet sailors enjoyed 123g of vodka and salt cabbage daily – is on display below decks. The museum also shows off the red flag which was raised on the night of the Revolution, as well as period uniforms and weaponry, songs composed in the ship's honour and gifts from various foreign communist dignitaries dating from the heyday of Soviet Bloc *bonhomie*.

Petrovskaya Naberezhnaya 4. Tel: 230 5202. Open: Monday to Friday 10.30am–4pm. Free. Metro: Gorkovskaya.

CANALS AND WATERWAYS

The struggle against an inhospitable environment and Peter the Great's fascination with Amsterdam combined to create one of the world's most beautiful maritime cities, defined by the flow of the Neva and drained on the south bank by a series of concentric canals and rivers.

St Petersburg's *raison d'être* was to open Russia to sea trade with Europe. When in November 1703 the first ship was sighted sailing down the Neva, a Dutch merchant vessel, Peter was so overjoyed that he rowed out to pilot it in personally before buying up the whole payload of wine and salt and rewarding the captain with 500 gold roubles. When the latter explained that he had intended to stop at the Swedish port of Narva, Peter promptly offered him another 300 roubles to quickly return.

At times the elements proved too powerful for the city's canals. Catherine the Great awoke on the morning of the great flood of 1777 to be informed that her wing of the Winter Palace was about to be submerged. 'Tell the guards in the courtyards that they may go home,' she replied. 'Otherwise, they will feel obliged to fight the onslaught of the waters and will likely get themselves killed.'

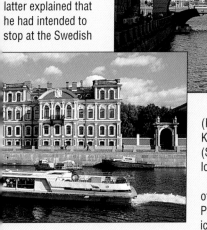

St Petersburg's waterways offer enchanting views of the city. A journey down the Griboyedova (formerly the Catherine) Canal leaves the onion domes of Khram Spasa 'Na Krovi' (Church of the Saviour 'on the Blood') behind as the boat passes beneath Nevskiy Prospekt and approaches the colonnades of Kazanskiy Sobor (Kazan Cathedral) before intersecting the Kryukova Canal at Nikolskiy Sobor (Sailors' Church of St Nicholas), a much-loved beauty spot.

For others, the quintessential image of St Petersburg will always be the Winter Palace shimmering in the frost before the icy patchwork of the frozen Neva.

See page 138 for details of canal and river rides.

Left: Griboyedova Canal. Above Fontanka Canal.
Above right: Bridge of Whispers

Churches and Cathedrals

*A*lthough not as rich in religious architecture as Moscow, St Petersburg boasts a fine collection of churches and cathedrals. Reflecting the city's conscious western orientation, many of them are a far cry from the squat, onion-domed constructions typical of the capital.

The best of the churches and cathedrals not mentioned elsewhere in the text are listed below.

(For a note on church etiquette, see page 37.)

BUDDIYSKIY KHRAM
(Buddhist Temple)

For sheer curiosity value, St Petersburg's one and only Buddhist temple is hard to beat. An entomological institute until lately, it was erected at the beginning of the century by one of the tsar's doctors who happened to be taken with Tibetan Buddhism. It has been returned to Russia's indigenous Buddhists, the Buryat tribe of Siberia, and is fully functional.

Primorskiy Prospekt 91. Tel: 239 1341. Metro: Chernaya Rechka then bus 94 or 166 to Lipovaya Alleya.

CHESMENSKAYA TSERKOV
(Chesme Church)

St Petersburg's most remarkable church is the neo-Gothic confection built by Yuri Felten to commemorate the defeat of the Turkish fleet near Chesma in 1770. Its arresting red and white candy-striped design, capped by pinnacles and lanterns, makes it quite unlike any other building in the country. The interior, a branch of the Naval Museum, contains an exhibition devoted to the famous victory. *Ulitsa Lensoveta 14–16. Metro: Moskovskaya.*

KNYAZ-VLADIMIRSKIY SOBOR
(Cathedral of Prince Vladimir)

This five-domed baroque construction looks a little the worse for wear, but is worth a visit for its unusually decorated interior, especially if you are visiting the nearby Dostoevsky Museum (see page 107). Despite repair works, it holds daily services.
Ulitsa Blokhina 16. Tel: 232 7625. Metro: Vladimirskaya.

Not part of a Russian Disneyland, but the extraordinary 18th-century Chesme Church

SAMPSONIEVSKIY SOBOR
(St Sampson's Cathedral)

One of the city's oldest buildings, the cathedral goes back to 1709 and Peter the Great's victory over the Swedes at Poltava on St Sampson's Day. Court gossip marked it as the scene of the secret wedding in 1774 between Catherine the Great and one of her lovers, Prince Potemkin. The original wooden structure was replaced by the newly-restored blue, green and white stone cathedral which opened in 1740.
Bolshoy Sampsonievskiy Prospekt 41. Metro: Vyborgskaya.

SPASO-PREOBRAZHENSKIY SOBOR (Cathedral of the Transfiguration)

Originally, this was the regimental church of the feared Preobrazhenskiy Guard, whose support was the key to the success of many a court intrigue and king/queen-making plot. The cathedral was a gift to the guards by a grateful Empress Elizabeth after one such incident. The building you see today dates from the late 1820s; Elizabeth's was razed by a fire in 1825.

Preobrazhenskaya Ploshchad 1. Tel: 272 3662. Metro: Chernyshevskaya.

TSERKOV IOANA PREDTECHI
(Church of John the Baptist)

Another of Felten's Gothic creations, the church was built in 1776 but spent much of the Soviet period as a basketball court. It has recently reopened for services.
Kamennoostrovskiy Prospekt 7. Metro: Petrogradskaya then bus 46.

THE ICON

Central to the Orthodox tradition, iconography can seem to outsiders close to superstition. Apparent contradiction of the commandment forbidding worship of graven images even led to a movement – iconoclasm – to destroy icons. But according to Orthodox doctrine, it is the reality represented rather than the icon itself that is venerated. Strict rules of composition deny flights of heretical fancy: the artist's goal is to balance pictorial representation and religious experience, evoking through the icon spiritual communion between subject and observer. This indefinable mystical contact and not the frequently primitive form is what Russians value in the works of masters like Andrei Rublev and Theophanes the Greek.

Dvortsovaya Ploshchad
(Palace Square)

*T*he footsteps of Imperial Guards and revolutionary detachments no longer echo across the square, yet this stage on which the drama of Russian history has played still readily conjures up its restless past.

Enclosed by the Winter Palace and the General Staff building, Palace Square was the tsars' favourite military parade ground. It was also the epicentre of the revolutions that condemned them to what Trotsky contemptuously referred to as 'the rubbish bin of history'.

The 1905 revolution flared when a crowd marched on the square petitioning Nicholas II to improve living and working conditions. Hundreds were killed when guards opened fire on the peaceful demonstrators, fatally wounding the weak tsar's image as the people's 'Little Father'.

On 25 October 1917, night of the Bolshevik Revolution, the square was the scene of the capture of the Winter Palace by Red Guards under Trotsky's command (see pages 12–13). The American journalist John Reed asked an opposition politician whether the insurrection would succeed: 'The devil knows!' he replied. 'Well, perhaps the Bolsheviks can seize power, but they won't be able to hold it more than three days ... Perhaps it's a good thing to let them try – that will finish them ...'

ALEKSANDROVSKAYA KOLONNA (Alexander Column)
The inscription on this monument to the defeat of Napoleon reads: 'To Alexander the First from a Grateful Russia.' It took over a year to haul the 700-tonne monolith, at 47.5m high the largest of its kind in the world, from a Finnish quarry

to St Petersburg. Over 2,000 soldiers and war veterans, cheered on by a huge crowd and watched by Nicholas I, pulled it on to the pedestal where it remains.

GLAVNIY SHTAB (General Staff building)
The approach to Palace Square from Bolshaya Morskaya Ulitsa is dominated by the triple arch of the General Staff building. The magnificent view of the square and Alexander Column thus created was the achievement of one of the city's greatest architects, Carlo Rossi (1775–1849). Apart from the bronze Chariot of Victory crowning the arch, the building is severely plain – befitting its subsequent role after the Revolution as headquarters of the city Cheka, forerunner of the KGB.

ZIMNIY DVORETS (Winter Palace)
The tsars' stunning winter residence, the fourth such palace on the site, was completed by Bartolomeo Rastrelli in 1762. It is considered the masterpiece of Russian baroque architecture, Rastrelli's genius lying in the skill with which he imbued the daunting 200m façade with such playful exuberance.

Most of the interior, apart from the elegant

RUSSIAN ROYALTY

1276–1303 Daniel	1598–1605 Boris	1730–40 Anna
1303–25 Yuri Danilolvich	Godunov	Iovannovna
1325–40 Ivan Kalita	1605–13 The 'Time of	1740–1 Ivan VI
1340–53 Simon the Proud	Troubles' – no clear ruler	1741–61 Elizabeth
1353–9 Ivan II	1613–45 Mikhail	1761–2 Peter III
1359–89 Dmitri Donskoy	Romanov	1762–96 Catherine
1389–1425 Vasili I	1645–76 Alexei Romanov	the Great
1425–62 Vasili the Dark	1676–82 Fedor	1796–1801 Paul
1462–1505 Ivan the	Alexeyevich	1801–25 Alexander I
Great	1682–9 Ivan V	1825–55 Nicholas I
1505– 33 Vasili III	1689–1725 Peter the Great	1855–81 Alexander II
1533–84 Ivan the Terrible	1725–7 Catherine I	1881–94 Alexander III
1584–98 Fedor Ivanovich	1727–30 Peter II	1894–1917 Nicholas II

Jordan Staircase, has been remodelled since Rastrelli's time according to the whim of passing tsars. The palace was almost entirely burnt to the ground in the fire of December 1837 but was completely rebuilt by Easter 1839.

Its staggeringly opulent state rooms and halls now function as what is probably the world's most luxurious art gallery, the State Hermitage Museum (see pages 98–101), which expanded from its adjoining annexe in 1922. *Metro: Nevskiy Prospekt, then trolleybus 1 or 7.*

The General Staff Building on Palace Square

Ermitazh
(State Hermitage Museum)

*T*his is one of the world's truly great art collections. The sheer volume (over 3 million) and quality of the exhibits makes it impossible to do them justice in a brief visit, and many travellers to St Petersburg come especially to devote their stay to the Hermitage's endless corridors and untold riches.

The story of the Hermitage begins with Peter the Great who brought back paintings from foreign tours and showed them in his Kunstkammer (see page 108). But it was during the reign of Catherine the Great that the collection really took shape. In 1764 she received 225 works from Frederick the Great of Prussia in lieu of payment for a debt and ordered her diplomats to seek more. The collections of Baron de Thiers and the British prime minister, Sir Robert Walpole, which she acquired, included large numbers of European masters.

Catherine allowed only selected guests to view the works, and it was not until after the 1917 Revolution that the doors of the Hermitage opened to the general public, when the museum was greatly expanded by confiscated private collections. As a specified German target, the museum's treasures were evacuated to the Urals during World War II. Today the greatest threat is disrepair and damp as the museum administration struggles with chronic underfunding. *Dvortsovaya Naberezhnaya 34. Tel: 219 8625. Open: 10.30am–6pm. Closed: Monday. Admission charge. Tours available in English. Metro: Nevskiy Prospekt, then trolleybuses 1 or 7.*

Viewing the collection

To spend just one minute looking at each of the exhibits would take over 12 years, so a visit should be planned carefully to avoid severe picture fatigue. The box opposite outlines the main order of the exhibition which occupies the former Winter Palace (entered through the chief Neva embankment entrance) and the Small and Large Hermitages. Some rooms are periodically closed for renovation and exhibits are often on fundraising tours.

The Special Collection and Hermitage Theatre

The ground floor of the Large Hermitage is also home to the museum's

Left: viewing the collection.
Opposite: the Hermitage from St Isaac's Cathedral

Special Collection, the highlight of which is an exhibition of Scythian gold jewellery. Dating from the 7th century BC, it contains incredibly ornate items of gold filigree work made by Black Sea tribes. Other exhibits include priceless jewel-incrusted articles belonging to the Russian Imperial Court.

The Hermitage Theatre, reached by an enclosed bridge over the Zimnaya Kanavka (Winter Canal), used to be Peter the Great's Winter Palace. It displays the results of excavations on the site, revealing in reconstructions Peter's modest lifestyle. *Entrance to both is restricted to groups. Separate tickets are sold at the Excursion Bureau up the steps to the right of the main ticket offices.*

Temporary exhibitions

The Hermitage hosts temporary exhibitions, advertised in the foyer. One that the administration hopes to make permanent is a display of European masterpieces stolen from Germany by the Red Army at the end of World War II. The hoard included canvases by Van Gogh, Cézanne and Gauguin, now on show for the first time in decades.

The State Rooms

The State Rooms of the tsars' Winter Palace are a breathtaking display of Imperial elegance. The Jordan Staircase, left from the ticket offices, leads majestically to the Antechamber, Nicholas Hall and Concert Hall before you arrive at the Malachite Room (189) where the Provisional Government convened before they were ousted by the Bolsheviks in the 1917 Revolution.

Below: nowhere are pictures displayed in more splendour. Opposite: the Malachite Room

Alternatively, turn right at the top of the staircase and head through the Field Marshall's Hall to Peter's Throne Room and the Armorial Hall. A door to the left leads to the 1812 Corridor, lined with paintings of the field commanders who defeated Napoleon, and through to the magnificent St George's Hall (198), adorned with a mosaic map of the USSR set with semi-precious stones.

Prehistory and antiquity

Occupying much of the ground floor, the Hermitage's collection includes a number of Egyptian mummies and sarcophagi and a display of classical artefacts – delicate cameos, terracotta figurines, mosaics, fine statuary ...

Russian art and culture

This section is devoted mostly to ceramics and furniture, old books and archaeological finds (Russian painting is largely confined to the Russian Museum – see pages 114–15).

Highlights of the Picture Gallery

Just a few delights to look out for among the countless paintings are listed below.

Italian

Madonna and Child with SS Dominic and Thomas Aquinas by Fra Angelico, room 209.
Madonna with a Flower and *Madonna and Child* by Leonardo da Vinci, room 214.
Danae and *The Penitent Mary Magdalene* by Titian, room 221.
Lamentation by Paolo Veronese, room 222.

Spanish

The Apostles Peter and Paul by El Greco, room 240.
The Luncheon by Diego Velázquez, room 239.
Portrait of Antonia Zarate by Francisco Goya, room 239.

Dutch and Flemish

The Adoration of the Magi and *Kermis* by Pieter Brueghel the Younger, room 262.

Perseus and Andromeda, *Feast at the House of Simon the Pharisee* and *Bacchus* by Peter Paul Rubens, room 247.
Charles I and *Virgin with Partridges* by Anthony Van Dyck, room 246.
Danae, *Abraham Sacrificing Isaac* and *The Return of the Prodigal Son* by Rembrandt, room 254.

French

Tancred and Erminia and *Landscape with Polyphemus* by Nicolas Poussin, room 279.
The Stolen Kiss by Jean-Honoré Fragonard, room 288.

English

The Infant Heracles Killing Snakes by Joshua Reynolds, room 299.
Portrait of a Lady in Blue by Thomas Gainsborough, room 300.

Modern European Art

Don't miss the wonderful collection of Impressionist and Post-Impressionist works and of canvases by Picasso and Matisse. The latter are owed to two Russian philanthropists who kept the artists solvent early in their careers.
After the Bath by Edgar Degas, room 320.
Still Life with Curtain and *The Smoker* by Paul Cézanne, room 318.
A Lady in the Garden and *Haystack at Giverny* by Claude Monet, room 319.
Portrait of the Actress Jeanne Samary by Auguste Renoir, room 320.
The Lilac Bush and *Cottages* by Vincent Van Gogh, room 317.
Woman holding a Fruit by Paul Gauguin, room 316.
The Dance and *Portrait of Mme Henri Matisse* by Henri Matisse, rooms 347–8.
The Absinthe Drinker and *Sisters* by Pablo Picasso, rooms 344–5.

The mighty dome of St Isaac's Cathedral was inspired by that of St Paul's in London ...

ISAAKIEVSKIY SOBOR
(St Isaac's Cathedral)

Monument to imperial self-confidence, the imposing bulk of St Isaac's Cathedral rises majestically on the St Petersburg skyline, its grand dome visible from far out in the Gulf of Finland.

The cathedral is named after the patron saint of the Romanov dynasty, St Isaac of Dalmatia, whose feast day coincides with Peter the Great's birthday. Peter was married in the city's first St Isaac's, a small wooden church constructed near the Admiralty (Admiralteystvo). The current cathedral is the fourth version, begun in 1818 by order of Alexander I following the defeat of the French.

Auguste de Montferrand

The building was the life's work of an unknown French architect, Auguste de Montferrand (1786–1858). Having moved to St Petersburg after service in Napoleon's army, he was the unlikely winner of the competition to redesign St Isaac's. His relative inexperience made him easy prey to the authoritarian tastes of Nicholas I expressed in the final product. The tsar declined his widow's request that the architect be buried in the cathedral, but a small bust of Montferrand, together with his original models, is on display in the nave.

Imperial splendour

St Isaac's impresses less by its design, which is architecturally uninspired, than by sheer mass and wealth of decoration. By the time it was completed in 1858, construction of the cathedral over 40 years had consumed more than 23 million roubles. Red granite was transported from Finland for the columns while the porticos were topped with dramatic bronze reliefs. Inside, over 200kg of gold went into gilding, white marble and lapis lazuli created a unique iconostasis, and the greatest artists of the day were commissioned to paint the interior frescos.

St Paul's Cathedral in London inspired the dome. Climbing the 262 steps to the colonnade affords a breathtaking panorama over St Petersburg's rooftops and the Neva beyond (separate ticket required). *Isaakievskaya Ploshchad 1. Tel: 315 9732. Open: 11am–6pm (colonnade till 5pm). Closed: Wednesday. Admission charge. Metro: Nevskiy Prospekt then trolleybus 14 or 22.*

Kazan' icon, was the fruit of his conviction that some day he would become Pope. In the event, he was assassinated by his exasperated courtiers.

Religion and politics
As a nationalist gesture, Paul ordered that a Russian architect be found to design the cathedral. Andrei Voronikhin, who was born a serf, completed his colonnaded masterpiece in 1811.

Paul's other obsession was militarism, and statues of his heroes, Generals Kutuzov and Barclay de Tolly, stand

... whereas the Kazan Cathedral, brainchild of Tsar Paul I, resembles St Peter's in Rome

KAZANSKIY SOBOR
(Kazan Cathedral)
One of the city's most striking buildings is the Kazan Cathedral on Nevskiy Prospekt, the design of which says more about the madness of its inspirer, Paul I, than it does of prevailing Orthodox taste.

The resemblance between the Kazan Cathedral and St Peter's in the Vatican is no accident: Paul I's slide into mental illness coincided with his obsession with the idea that he could unite the Catholic and Orthodox faiths. The cathedral, named after the venerated 'Virgin of

guard in the square. Inside the cathedral, Kutuzov's tomb is in the north chapel where he prayed to the famous icon before battle. The icon itself vanished mysteriously before the Revolution.

Under the Soviets, the Cathedral became the Museum of Atheism, full of gory Inquisition exhibits 'proving' the falseness of religion. It now houses the comparatively dull 'museum of religion'. *Kazanskaya Ploshchad 2. Tel: 311 0495. Open: 11am–5pm (from noon at weekends). Closed: Wednesday. Metro: Nevskiy Prospekt. Admission charge.*

THE NEXT GENERATION

Childhood in communist Russia was a highly-structured affair, aiming to turn out fine specimens of *Homo sovieticus*. For those who wanted to succeed there was only one way forward.

Youngsters joined the Oktyabryata – 'Little Octoberites' – before spending summer holidays at 'Pioneer' camps, where traditional scouting was accompanied by lessons in Marxism-Leninism. Together with members of the Komsomol, the youth wing of the Communist Party, the chosen would wave banners and march in Revolution Day parades before being groomed for the Party membership essential to gaining a powerful job.

Education was free, but for access to top universities and institutes you needed influential relations, an example of *blat* – 'friends in high places' – without whom life was an uphill struggle. Sons and daughters of 'enemies of the

watches to tourists on Red Square. Teenagers throw themselves into studying foreign languages in the hopes of joining western multinationals.

But as old certainties vanish, many feel trapped by freedoms they are ill-equipped to exploit. Cult religions flourish in Moscow and St Petersburg, preying on those adrift in the chaos. Others turn to alcohol or home-made drugs. Young girls know that they can make many times the average yearly wage in a week's work as a hard-currency

Some still adhere to discipline (above), but the breakdown of the old order has, on the whole, given freedom to the young

people' and Jews could count on life being harder still.

Now the rules of the game have changed and the youth of Moscow and St Petersburg are at the cutting edge of Russia's new revolution. Many of the new generation of sharp-suited securities dealers and commodities traders cut their market teeth selling rabbit-fur hats and military

prostitute. Illegal brothels in the capital have grown from a few dozen in 1992 to well over a thousand. And those unable to fathom the intricacies of big business can earn as much and more working for organised crime.

Literary St Petersburg

St Petersburg is crammed with small museums, memorials and obscure back alleys, familiar to readers even today from pages written about the city a century or more ago.

ALEXANDER PUSHKIN

Pushkin (1799–1837) is considered the country's greatest man of letters, credited with inventing literary Russian. His appeal is universal – one 19th-century critic neatly called him 'Our all'.

Born in Moscow, he was educated at the Imperial Lyceum in Tsarskoe Selo (see page 130) and in 1820 published his first poem *Ruslan and Ludmilla* to huge acclaim. His mentor Zhukovsky presented the young poet with a portrait inscribed 'To the victorious pupil from the vanquished master' which hangs in his study, preserved in the Pushkin House Museum. On his desk stands an African figurine to remind him of his Abyssinian forebear, given to Peter the Great by the Russian ambassador to Constantinople and the subject of his final, unfinished work.

The clock in the study is stopped at 2.45am, the time of Pushkin's death following a duel for the honour of his beautiful wife, Natalia Goncharova. Pushkin met his opponent, a salon dandy named D'Anthès, outside the city at Chernaya Rechka. The spot is marked by a monument at the end of Novosibirskaya Ulitsa (*metro: Chernaya Rechka*).

Muzey-Kvartira A S Pushkina (Pushkin House Museum), Reki Moyki Naberezhnaya 12. Tel: 311 3801. Open: 10.30am–6.30pm. Closed: Tuesday and last Friday of the month. Admission charge. Metro: Nevskiy Prospekt.

FYODOR DOSTOEVSKY

Dostoevsky (1821–88), the acknowledged master of the depths of the human soul, found the inspiration for his novel *Crime and Punishment* among the slums of St Petersburg's Haymarket – Sennaya Ploshchad – basing its hero, Raskolnikov, in lodgings at nearby Grazhdanskaya Ulitsa 19. While he wrote it, he lived in the next street,

Revered by Russians, Alexander Pushkin

Kaznacheyskaya Ulitsa 7 (*metro: Sennaya Ploshchad*). The old woman killed by Raskolnikov's axe is supposed to have lived on the Griboyedova Canal embankment at No 104.

Earlier associations with socialists had brought the author eight months' imprisonment in the Peter-and-Paul fortress (see page 110) before being lined up for execution on Zagorodniy Prospekt, then a military parade ground (*metro: Pushkinskaya*). The sentence was commuted to four years' labour in Siberia, which inspired his account of the tsarist Gulag in *The House of the Dead*.

Dostoevsky's final home, where he wrote *The Brothers Karamazov*, is open to visitors. Russian films of his works are shown on the ground floor.
Muzey-Kvartira F M Dostoevskovo (Dostoevsky House-Museum), Kuznechniy Pereulok 5/2. Tel: 164 6950. Open: 10.30am–5pm. Closed: Monday and last Wednesday of the month. Admission charge. Metro: Vladimirskaya.

Other points on the literary map

Her husband executed by the Bolsheviks, her son imprisoned, her works unprinted most of her life, Anna Akhmatova (1889–1966) remained one of Russia's most human poetesses. Her rooms have been converted into an illuminating museum.
Muzey A Akhmatova, Reki Fontanki Naberezhnaya 34, entry through Liteyniy Prospekt 53. Tel: 272 2211. Open: 10.30am–6.30pm. Closed: Monday and last Wednesday of the month. Admission charge. Metro: Gostiniy Dvor.

The émigré writer Vladimir Nabokov, author of *Lolita*, grew up at Ulitsa Bolshaya Morskaya 47 (*metro: Nevskiy*

The Literaturnoe Kafe, meeting-place of Pushkin and his second before the fatal duel

Prospekt). Near by, at Ulitsa Malaya Morskaya 17, Nikolai Gogol (1809–52) wrote his comedy *The Government Inspector* and much of his sombre opus *Dead Souls*.

The Literary Institute, affectionately known as Pushkinskiy Dom (Pushkin House), on the Strelka, is packed with priceless items, from medieval religious texts to Byron's poems, Queen Victoria's letters and Mozart's manuscripts. It is temporarily closed to the public but the truly keen may gain admittance.
Naberezhnaya Makarova 4. Tel: 218 0502. Metro: Nevskiy Prospekt, then trolleybus 1 or 7.

Museums

St Petersburg is home to a wealth of museums, some of them excellent, some a little dusty and outdated – and some simply weird.

ISTORICHESKIY MUZEY VOSKOVYKH FIGUR (Historical Waxworks Museum)

The waxworks illustrating key figures and events of modern Russian history are in the annexe of what was once the highly orthodox Museum of the Revolution. In the former mansion of *prima ballerina* (and tsar's mistress) Matilda Kschessinskaya (1872–1971), the museum now displays up-to-date and frank exhibitions on the country's recent history.

Ulitsa Kuybysheva 2/4. Tel: 233 7189. Open: 10am–6pm, Friday to Wednesday; waxworks daily. Admission charge. Metro: Gorkovskaya.

LITERARY AND WRITERS' HOUSE MUSEUMS

See pages 106–7.

MUZEY ANTROPOLOGII I ETNOGRAFII (Museum of Anthropology and Ethnography)

The highlight of this museum is Peter the Great's collection of curiosities, (formerly known as the Kunstkammer), one of St Petersburg's oldest sights. Thankfully no longer offering live exhibits, it contains pickled mutants, both human and animal, which caught the tsar's fancy and for which he paid handsomely. Bottled Siamese twins, hairy babies and two-faced embryos are displayed alongside selected vital organs.

Universitetskaya Naberezhnaya 3. Tel: 218 1412. Open: Thursday to Tuesday 11am–4.45pm. Admission charge. Metro: Nevskiy Prospekt.

MUZEY ETNOGRAFII (Ethnography Museum)

Located in the same building as the Russian Museum (see pages 114–15), the Mikhailovsky Palace, this museum is devoted to the peoples of the former USSR, illustrating the patchwork of nationalities with waxworks, tableaux and various archaeological paraphernalia.

Inzhenernaya Ulitsa 4/1. Tel: 210 3888. Open: Tuesday to Sunday 10am–6pm. Closed: Monday and the last Friday of the month. Admission charge. Metro: Nevskiy Prospekt.

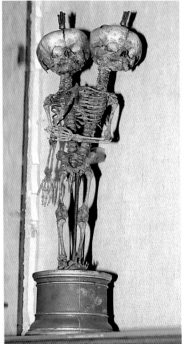

Siamese twins, one of Peter the Great's curiosities

Wartime poster in the Museum of the Defence of Leningrad

MUZEY GIGIYENY
(Hygiene Museum)

This horrific assortment of pickled and diseased parts of the body and graphic posters is worth a visit – if only to learn what Leningrad schoolchildren were forced to look at to keep them clean-living, wholesome Soviet citizens.

Italianskaya Ulitsa 25. Tel: 210 8508. Open: Monday to Friday 10am–5pm. Free. Metro: Nevskiy Propsekt.

MUZEY S M KIROVA
(Kirov Museum)

Entering the apartment of Lenigrad party chief Sergei Kirov is like stepping back in time – not only for the period furnishings but also for the reverence in which both Kirov and Stalin are still held by the elderly wardens. Kirov's bullet-holed cap and recordings of Stalin haranguing the masses are among the exhibits.

Kamennoostrovskiy Prospekt 26/28. Tel: 233 3822. Open: Thursday to Tuesday 11am–6pm. Admission charge. Metro: Gorkovskaya.

MUZEY OBORONY LENINGRADA
(Museum of the Defence of Leningrad)

This provides a fascinating insight into the horrors of Leningrad's 872 days of siege in World War II (see page 111). Apart from telling the tale of daily survival, it also exhibits art produced during the blockade.

Solanoy Pereulok 9. Tel: 275 7208. Open: Thursday to Tuesday 10am–5pm. Admission charge. Metro: Chernyshevskaya.

VOENNO MORSKOY MUZEY
(Naval Museum)

Dioramas and intricate models tell the story of the development of Russia's fleet from landlocked impotence to Cold War technical wizardry. Don't miss Peter the Great's tiny rowing boat..

Birzhevaya Ploshchad 4. Tel: 218 3623. Open: Wednesday to Sunday. Closed: Monday, Tuesday and last Thursday of the month) 10.30am–5.30pm. Admission charge. Metro: Nevskiy Prospekt.

ZOOLOGICHESKIY MUZEY
(Zoological Museum)

Pride of place among the stuffed birds and animals is occupied by Siberian mammoths (when they are not on tour). One has lost part of its trunk – eaten by the dogs of the expedition that found it!

Universitetskaya Naberezhnaya 1. Tel: 218 0112. Open: Thursday to Tuesday 11am–5pm. Admission charge. Metro: Nevsiky Prospekt.

PETROPAVLOVSKAYA KREPOST (Peter-and-Paul Fortress)

Its grim walls squatting 18m thick on the Neva Delta, this stronghold was erected in a matter of months by press-ganged peasants to fend off Swedish designs on Peter the Great's 'window on to Europe'. Graced by the stiletto spire of the Cathedral of SS Peter and Paul rising behind the ramparts, the fortress became a city landmark ... and the darkest of imperial political gaols.

Peter the Great's tomb in the Cathedral of SS Peter and Paul is marked by a bust of the tsar

Petropavlovskiy Sobor (Cathedral of SS Peter and Paul)

The unashamedly Protestant design of St Petersburg's first church underlines Peter's determination to found a crucible of westernisation even at the expense of Orthodox church opinion.

Within, most of Russia's tsars and tsarinas, from Peter on, lie in sarcophagi amid the baroque splendour. Peter's tomb is to the right of the lavish iconostasis. His son Alexei is said to be buried beneath the belltower staircase – to suffer the ignominy of being trampled on for eternity. A passage on the left leads to a mausoleum where the remains of Nicholas II's family, murdered in the Urals, are likely soon to be interred.

Trubetskoy Bastion

Crossing the cathedral courtyard (the unmarked site of Bolshevik firing squads), note the Monetniy Dvor (Mint) – still operational – before entering tsarism's dreaded Trubetskoy Bastion. Tsarevich Alexei, eventually beaten to

PETER THE GREAT (1672–1725)

Fired by travels abroad in his youth, Peter modelled his court on Versailles, streamlined the bureaucracy and championed industrialisation. But despite his passion for reason in a country steeped in superstition, Peter had a strong streak of the barbarian in him. Soirées at the Summer Palace dissolved into gothic debauchery. St Petersburg was constructed, much as Stalin's projects were, by sheer effort of will and drastic loss of life. Capable of extreme cruelty, Peter personally saw to the torture of Alexei, his only son.

Like Gorbachev, Peter was adored by westernisers but was similarly motivated less by love of the 'effete' west than by the need to make the Russian system work better, remarking : 'We shall need Europe for a few decades and then we can show her our backside!'.

death as a suspected traitor, was the first of many 'enemies of the state' incarcerated here, including Alexander II's assassins, Trotsky and Lenin's brother Alexander. Nobody escaped.

Reading and writing were outlawed and total isolation was enforced: guards were forbidden to speak to or know the identity of inmates and patrolled soundproofed corridors. Insubordination meant the *kartser* or cooler (literally – it was unheated in winter); mere rudeness to the guards merited two days' darkness.

Museums and exhibitions
The Komandantskiy Domik (Commandant's House) and Inzhenirniy Korpus (Engineer's House) display exhibitions of city history, while near the entrance the Museum of Gas Dynamics, full of space-race memorabilia, was once a top secret rocket laboratory.

Across the river from Winter Palace. Tel: 238 4540. Open: Thursday to Tuesday 11am–6pm. Closed: Wednesday and last Tuesday of the month. Tickets from kassa through Ivan Gates on Troitskiy Bridge entrance. All sights well signposted. Metro: Gorkovskaya.

DOMIK PETRA (Peter's Cabin)
Close by is the original wooden cabin from which Peter supervised the fortress's construction in the summer of 1703. The three spartan rooms vividly evoke the frontier spirit of the times. Note Peter's study and the pipe on the table – smoking, like his tax on beards, was a law-enforced element of the tsar's assault on Russian 'backwardness'.
Petrovskaya Naberezhnaya 6. Tel: 238 0070. Open: 10am–6pm. Closed: Wednesday. Admission charge. Metro: Gorkovskaya.

PISKARYOVSKOE MEMORIALNOE KLADBISHCHE (Piskaryovskoe Memorial Cemetery)
Ranks of mass graves stretch 300m out from the cemetery's eternal flame, solemn testimony to that most horrifying episode, the Siege of Leningrad.

The Siege
As the first shells landed in September 1941, Hitler's order was 'to wipe the city of Petersburg from the face of the earth'. The ensuing blockade lasted 872 days.

The Nazis failed to take the city, but Leningraders endured colossal suffering. Some 670,000 died, the majority of starvation. By December 1941 the bread ration was set at 255g daily for troops and workers, half that for ordinary citizens. The fortunate survived on supplies brought across the precarious 'Road of Life' spanning frozen Lake Ladoga; others turned to cannibalism.

Many of the city's 3,200 bombed-out buildings were lovingly restored, but the ordeal is still alive in the memory of the many lonely *babushkas* selling beer at metro stations late into the night.

The Cemetery
Weakened by hunger, the citizens of Leningrad abandoned digging individual graves and gathered bodies in mass pits near the hamlet of Piskaryovka. The site was reorganised after the war with a simple slab set on each grave – marked with a star for soldiers, otherwise with an oak leaf and hammer and sickle. At the far end, the inscription on the wall concludes simply: 'Let no one forget. Let no one be forgotten.' Memorial halls at the gates contain a poignant exhibition.
Prospekt Nepokoryonnykh. Tel: 247 5716. Open: daily 10am–6pm. Free. Metro: Ploshchad Muzhestva and then bus 123 or 131.

THE

The unhappy reign of the last of the Romanov dynasty, Tsar Nicholas II, started inauspiciously when 3,000 well-wishers were crushed in the crowd at his coronation in 1896. Later, he gained the nickname 'Bloody Nicholas' after hundreds of peaceful demonstrators petitioning for better conditions were massacred on Palace Square in 1905. But essentially Nicholas was a quiet, timid man, quite at odds with the stormy times besetting his country.

Devoted to his family and his sickly, haemophiliac son Alexis, the Emperor and Autocrat of all the Russias was thought by his cousin Kaiser Wilhelm better cut out to be a 'country gentleman growing turnips'. Despite growing civil unrest and mutinies in the fleet, he rarely involved himself in matters of state, preferring to spend most of the year at the royal retreat of Tsarskoe Selo.

Meanwhile his popularly despised German wife was besotted with the mystic monk Rasputin,

AST OF THE ROMANOVS

'others do when they make a list of dirty laundry'. On 2 March 1917, tsarism died in Russia.

Its resting place was to be a shallow grave near Ekaterinburg in the Urals where, in July the following year, the dismembered bodies of Nicholas, his family, servants and the pet spaniel were doused in sulphuric acid and dumped by Bolshevik secret police. The final order to blow up even the building where the murders were committed was given in 1977 by the then local party chief, Boris Yeltsin.

Opposite: Nicholas II riding out of the Kremlin, and the royal throne. Above: Nicholas and Alexandra. Right: their daughters

thought able to cure her son. Society was scandalised: Rasputin's lewd soirées were common knowledge yet his power over the royal family seemed total.

Finally, the exactions of a deeply unpopular war brought Russia to boiling point. Huge food riots rampaged through Petrograd. The army had revolted. Nicholas signed his abdication in a railway carriage in pencil as

Russkiy Muzey
(Russian Museum)

St Petersburg's superb collection of Russian art is comparable only with the Tretyakov Gallery in Moscow in quality and scale (see pages 66–7). The Russian Museum's rooms provide a journey through the development of painting in Russia, from the earliest iconography to the avant-garde explosion and subsequent Stalinist orthodoxy of the 20th century.

Iconography

A chronological tour starts on the first floor in rooms 1–4, containing fine examples of Russia's earliest art form, icon painting. One of the oldest is the 12th-century Archangel Gabriel, known as *Angel Golden-Hair* and reflecting Byzantine influences in the stylised rendition of the angel's features. Other highlights include an early icon of the murdered sons of Prince Vladimir, SS Boris and Gleb, a stunning 15th-century *St George and the Dragon*, and works by the acknowledged master of the genre, Andrei Rublev.

Art under Peter the Great

Russian art reached a watershed during the reign of Peter the Great. Thrilled by

'The Mother of God' in the Russian Museum

what he had seen in Europe, he sent his most promising artists abroad on scholarships to perfect their skills. The results are displayed in room 5: Ivan Nikitin's *Portrait of the Hetman* (1720?), and *Portrait of the Artist and his Wife* (1729?) by Andrei Matveev illustrate the break away from the medieval past.

Academy of Arts

Founded in 1757, the Academy of Arts advocated principles of classicism, emphasising subjects from history, the Bible and classical mythology. Room 9 shows an early history painting, *Vladimir and Rogneda* (1770) by Anton Losenko, depicting the horror of a Polovtsian princess after the murder of her father and brothers by her determined suitor, Prince Vladimir.

Leaps of progress in portraiture are demonstrated in room 10 with the work of Dmitri Levitsky, especially his canvases of *Count Vorontsov* (1780s) and Academy director *Alexander Kokorinov* (1769).

Of the early 19th-century classical paintings, the outstanding item is Karl Bryullov's monumental *Last Day of Pompeii* (1833) in room 15. Rooms 21–2 on the ground floor are devoted to the academy's other hero, Alexander Ivanov, studies for whose greatest work, *The Appearance of Christ before the People* (1857), are on display.

St Petersburg's Russian Museum contains some 315,000 items of Russian art in over 100 rooms

'The Wanderers'

The group of realist artists dubbed 'The Wanderers' (see page 60) was led by Ivan Kramskoy, whose piercing portraits fill room 25. Nikolai Ge scandalised society with the realism of his *Last Supper* (1863) in room 26. Another member, Ilya Repin, is one of Russia's best-loved painters and a large number of his works are hung in rooms 33–5. Two of his most famous canvases are *Barge-haulers on the Volga* (1873) and the hilarious *Zaporozhe Cossacks* (1891).

Turning the century

Russian art experienced an explosion of styles at the turn of the century. Isaak Levitan's wistful landscapes in room 38 demonstrate his mastery of impressionism; alongside is Mikhail Vrubel's *Azrail* (1904), a vibrant, haunting symbolist masterpiece. Philip Malyavin's richly coloured pictures of peasant women in room 39 defy easy classification.

The Benois Wing

This holds semi-permanent exhibitions from the museum's huge reserve of avant-garde and 'socialist realist' art. Among the works periodically on show are abstract compositions by Kazimir Malevich and Vasili Kandinsky, 'constructivist' designs by Vladimir Tatlin, and works by the founders of 'primitivism', Mikhail Larionov and Natalya Goncharova. You may also come across examples of graphic propaganda from the 1920s along with dull but officially sanctioned portraits of happy, square-jawed workers and painstaking renditions of Communist Party conferences.

Inzhenernaya Ulitsa 4. Tel: 219 1615. Open: Wednesday to Monday 10am–6pm (entrance to the right of the main steps). Tours available in English. Admission charge. Metro: Gostiniy Dvor. Entrance to the Benois Wing is from the Griboyedova Canal embankment.

Nevskiy Prospekt

St Petersburg's main thoroughfare, a pulsating
artery of shopping, busking, painting and
pickpocketing, is almost 5km long. Packed with
people from dawn till dusk, it is at its most
charming on a frosty winter morning or in the
eerie dusk of a June night.
Allow 1½ hours.

Begin at the Anichkov Most (Bridge) over the Fontanka river.

1 BELOSELSKIY-BELOZERSKIY DVORETS
(Beloselskiy-Belozerskiy Palace)

This rococo triumph, with its muscle-bound caryatids and
radiant crimson exterior, housed local Communist Party offices
until 1991. Before the Revolution, the palace was the residence
of the Governor of Moscow. The splendid interior is worth a
look.

*Cross the bridge and note the face of Nicholas I depicted by a
frustrated (and exceptionally brave) sculptor in the groin of one of
the horses.*

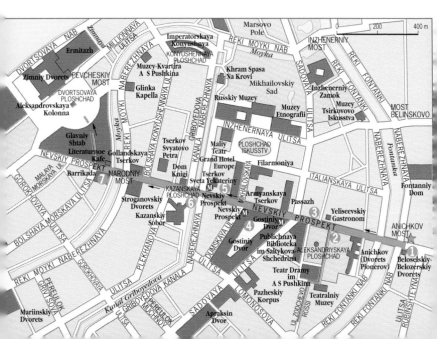

2 ALEKSANDRINSKAYA PLOSHCHAD

The square is dominated by the statue of Catherine the Great surrounded by her favourites, with Teatr Dramy im A S Pushkina (Pushkin Drama Theatre), Russia's oldest theatre, behind and Publichnaya Biblioteka im Saltykova-Shchedrina (the Russian National Library), where Lenin once studied, to her left. Down Ulitsa Zodchevo Rossi behind the theatre is the Vaganova Ballet School; Pavlova, Nijinsky and Nureyev were among its alumni. *Return to Nevskiy Prospekt and cross over.*

3 YELISEEVSKIY GASTRONOM

Across from the square is Yeliseev's, St Petersburg's finest victualler's. The interior retains much of its pre-revolutionary grandeur. Nationalised after 1917, the store was known, as plain 'Food Shop No 1'.

4 GOSTINIY DVOR

This 18th-century bazaar (the name means 'merchants' hostelries'), almost 1,000m in circumference, is presently being turned into a modern shopping arcade. The pavement outside is favoured by moneychangers and artists. *Continue past the old town hall with its red fire-tower and cross the street.*

5 ARMYANSKAYA TSERKOV AND TSERKOV SVETA YEKATERINY (Armenian Church and Catholic Church of St Catherine)

Non-Orthodox churches were allowed

Caryatids adorning the
Beloselskiy-Belozerskiy Palace

on Nevskiy Prospekt, giving it the sobriquet 'Street of Tolerance'. These two are both under restoration, the former having been used as a workshop. The nearby Lutheran church remains a municipal swimming pool for the time being.

6 KANAL GRIBOYEDOVA

Pause on the Kazan Bridge for a super view of Khram Spasa Na Krove (the Church on the Spilled Blood – see page 121) down the canal, and the magnificent columns of Kazanskiy Sobor (Kazan Cathedral – see page 103) across the street. On the right, the glass-domed building was the home of the Singer Sewing Machine Company. *Passing Stroganovskiy Dvorets (Stroganov Palace), whose chef invented the eponymous beef dish, cross the Narodniy Most.*

7 TO PALACE SQUARE

The Café Wulf et Béranger (now the Literaturnoe Kafe) was where the poet Pushkin met his second before his fatal duel in 1837 (see page 106). Note the sign at No 15 left over from the siege – 'Citizens! In the event of artillery fire, this side of the street is more dangerous!' Head along to Bolshaya Morskaya Ulitsa and enter Dvortsovaya Ploshchad (Palace Square – see page 96) through the triple arch of the General Staff building.

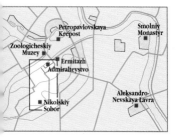

Neva West Bank to the Kanal Griboyedova

From god-forsaken port through imperial metropolis to unnerving haunt of historical spectres ... the district west of Palace Square captures the essence of St Petersburg. *Allow 2 hours.*

Start at the Admiralty at the end of Nevskiy Prospekt.

1 ADMIRALTEYSTVO (Admiralty)

Conceived as a naval stronghold, St Petersburg centres on

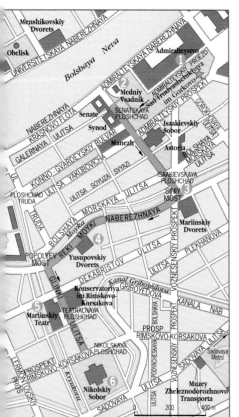

Andreyan Zakharov's Admiralty (1823), the apotheosis of Russian neo-classicism. Some 400m long, it dominates the site of Peter the Great's shipyards; its frigate weathervane became the city's symbol. *Walk through the Admiralty Gardens to Senatskaya Ploshchad (Senate Square).*

2 MEDNIY VSADNIK (The Bronze Horseman)

Until recently Senate Square was named after the failed 'Decembrist' uprising of army officers in 1825, when troops gathered at the far end of the square to demand constitutional reform. Nicholas I easily crushed the rebellion.

One sympathiser, the great poet Alexander Pushkin, escaped with a warning, surviving to pen his epic *The Bronze Horseman*, its title taken from the statue of Peter the Great in the square. *Turn away from the river and make for St Isaac's Cathedral.*

3 ISAAKIEVSKAYA PLOSHCHAD (St Isaac's Square)

Isaakievskiy Sobor (St Isaac's Cathedral – see page 102) gives its name to the square beyond it, much of which is a vast bridge over the Moyka river. Opposite is the Mariinskiy Dvorets (Mariinskiy Palace), currently the city council but originally built in 1844 for the daughter of Nicholas I, whose equestrian statue stands in the centre of the square.

On the east, the Astoria Hotel is where journalist John Reed (1887–1920) wrote his classic account of the Revolution, *Ten Days that Shook the World*.
Cross the Moyka and follow the embankment westwards.

4 YUSUPOVSKIY DVORETS
(Yusupov Palace)
No 94 was the residence of the fabulously rich Prince Felix Yusupov and scene of the 1916 assassination of Rasputin. Exasperated by the grip on the court of the 'mad monk' (see page 113), a group of aristocrats enticed him to Yusupov's basement for an evening of debauchery. Poisoned and0. shot in the head, Rasputin refused to die even when beaten and shot another four times. The terrified conspirators then threw him into the river where he drowned. You can visit the cellar, complete with waxworks.
Continue along the embankment and turn left on to Glinki Ulitsa to Teatralnaya Ploshchad.

5 MARIINSKIY TEATR
(Mariinskiy Theatre)
The square saw an explosion of talent at the turn of the century: the legendary dancers Anna Pavlova and Vaslav Nijinsky created a sensation at the Mariinskiy Theatre, while the nearby Conservatory (Konservatoriya im Rimskovo-Korsakova) nurtured the ground-breaking composers Dmitri Shostakovich and Igor Stravinsky. (See pages 60–1.)

Continue along Glinki Ulitsa to St Nicholas Cathedral.

6 NIKOLSKIY SOBOR
(St Nicholas Cathedral)
The proximity of sailors' barracks at the time of its construction explains why St Nicholas Cathedral is known as The Sailors' Church. The epitome of the baroque style preferred by Empress Elizabeth, it is at its most bewitching during the daily evening services.
Trams 14 and 54 run along Sadovaya Ulitsa to Sadovaya metro station.

The gilded spire of the Admiralty, with its weathervane in the form of a sailing ship

The Winter Palace to the Summer Garden

This short stroll encompasses the sites of two regicides, the home of Russia's greatest poet, two royal palaces and the Summer Garden. *Allow 2 hours.*

Start on the eastern side of Dvortsovaya Ploshchad (Palace Square, see pages 96–7).

1 THE RIVER MOYKA

Crossing Pevcheskiy Most (Singers' Bridge) to the right bank of the winding Moyka, you are faced with the Glinka Kapella, St

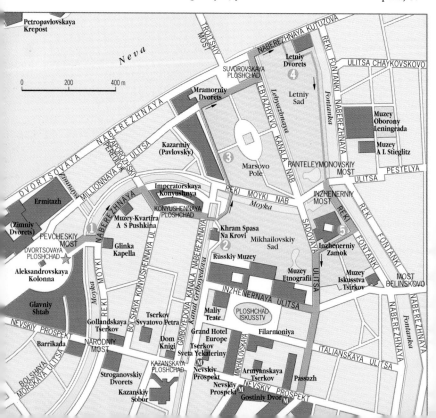

Petersburg's oldest concert hall and once headquarters of the celebrated Imperial Court Choir.

A little further on, at Reki Moyki Naberezhnaya 12, Russia's national poet Alexander Pushkin lived in the first floor apartments (open to visitors – see page 106). The poet's funeral took place in the Equerries' Church which occupies the central block of the Imperial Stables, commanding Konyushennaya Ploshchad to the right from the river.
Continue across the square to the bridge over the Griboyedova Canal

2 KHRAM SPASA NA KROVI (CHURCH ON THE SPILLED BLOOD)

St Petersburg's most incongruous church is a near copy of St Basil's Cathedral in Moscow, its Orthodox design reflecting the surge in nationalist feeling at the time. It commemorates the assassination of Alexander II; the altar stands over the place where the tsar was blown up by a revolutionary bomb in 1881 – hence 'on the spilled blood'. (Church closed.)
Head north, once more crossing the Moyka.

3 MARSOVO POLE (The Field of Mars)

The open expanse north of the Moyka became an imperial parade ground. The eternal flame in the centre honours the 180 dead of the 1917 February Revolution buried here, and the fallen of the October Revolution and Civil War.

The Mramorniy Dvorets (Marble Palace) of 1785 at the far end of the square was built for Catherine the Great's lover Count Grigori Orlov, who managed to lose it twice at cards.
Enter the Summer Garden through the beautiful wrought-iron grille from the embankment

4 LETNIY SAD AND LETNIY DVORETS (Summer Garden and Summer Palace)

The Summer Garden was laid out informally after a flood in 1777 washed away Peter the Great's more ambitious pastiche of the gardens of Versailles.

Peter's Summer Palace (1710) is characteristically modest. His wife lived on the first floor while Peter busied himself in the turnery or at raucous banquets below. The park is more tranquil than in Peter's day, when he would order the nobility to join in his compulsory 'drinking assemblies'.
Leaving the Summer Garden, take the Fontanka left bank to the Engineer's Castle

5 INZHENERNIY ZAMOK (Engineer's Castle)

The curious architecture of the Engineer's Castle (1801) was once surrounded by a moat to protect Paul I, terrified of assassination. He hurried the construction of his redoubt, plundering the site of the unfinished St Isaac's Cathedral. But Paul died mere days after he had moved in, throttled in his nightshirt by courtiers and army officers exasperated by their tsar's accelerating insanity. The building takes its name from the Engineering Academy to which it was transferred. (Closed.)
A short walk south brings you to Nevskiy Prospekt or Ploshchad Iskusstv and the Russian Museum (see pages 114-15).

Letniy Sad open: 8am–10pm (to 8pm in winter). Free.
Letniy Dvorets, tel: 314 0374. Open: 11am–7pm. Closed: Tuesday and May to 10 November. Admission charge.

Vasilevskiy Ostrov and the Strelka

The majestic view of the Neva delta from the tip of Vasilevskiy Island readily conjures up the dream of maritime grandeur that obsessed Peter the Great. Embracing some of the city's oldest buildings, the island's streets still evoke the breathtaking imperial self-confidence that fired the tsar's vision. *Allow 2 hours, excluding museum visits.*

Start at metro Vasileostrovskaya. Turn right down 6 and 7 Liniya.

1 TO BOLSHOY PROSPEKT

Make for the pink belltower of the Andreevskiy Sobor (Cathedral of St Andrew) of 1780, with a wonderful iconostasis in its lofty vaulted interior, and the picturesque, if dilapidated, Tserkov Tryokh Svyatitelyei (Church of Three Holy Men) behind.

Heading left along attractive Bolshoy Prospekt, note No 6 where Tatyana Savicheva, whose diary is exhibited at the

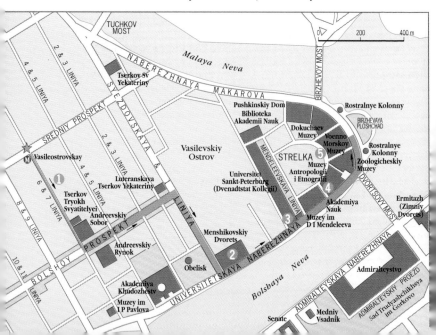

Piskaryovskoe Cemetery (see page 111), recorded the starvation of her family during the siege. The 1771 Luteranskaya Tserkov Sv Yekateriny (Lutheran Church of St Catherine) stands opposite, reopened following occupation by a Soviet-era record company.

Turn right on to 1 Liniya, passing to the left the former Imperial Cadet barracks, site of Lenin's first bid for power at the Soviet of Workers' and Soldiers' Deputies in June 1917. Turn left on to Universitetskaya Naberezhnaya.

2 MENSHIKOVSKIY DVORETS (Menshikov's Palace)

Ochre paintwork and Dutch-style gables characterise the palace built from 1710 to 1720 for Peter's friend and favourite Alexander Menshikov (1673–1729). Of humble background, he shared the tsar's earthy *joie de vivre* and won immense influence, ultimately becoming city governor.

The rooms inside have been carefully restored, the highlights being the tiled first-floor quarters, the lathe at which Peter amused himself, and the kitchen's enormous wooden beer vessel – big enough for the duo's fabled bawdy dinner parties.

Menshikov's luck turned after the deaths of Peter and his wife (Menshikov's former servant and mistress) Catherine I, and he died in Siberian exile, penniless.

3 DVENADTSTAT KOLLEGII (The Twelve Colleges)

Among Petersburg's oldest buildings, the Colleges were built for Peter's government bureaucracy. Given to the University in 1819, they became an epicentre of militancy. Lenin graduated from the law faculty, but soon

abandoned law to devote himself to revolution.

A statue of the great scholar Mikhail Lomonosov (1708–65) divides the Colleges from the neo-classical Akademiya Nauk (Academy of Sciences), outside which a plaque records the flood level when the Neva burst its banks in 1924.

Continue along the embankment.

4 MUZEY ANTROPOLOGII I ETNOGRAFII (Museum of Anthropology and Ethnography)

Peter's fascination with science led him during a trip to Holland to purchase the collection of anatomical oddities at the heart of Russia's first museum (1718). Free vodka enticed visitors to gaze at pickled bottled freaks that, over two and a half centuries on, have lost none of their power to shock. (See page 108.)

Return to the embankment passing the Zoological Museum (see page 109).

5 THE STRELKA

Commanding a superb view of Peter and Paul Fortress and the Winter Palace, the Strelka – or island spit – is a St Petersburg trademark, especially on public holidays when the two rostral columns are lit up at night.

The Stock Exchange, now the Voenno Morskoy Muzey (Naval Museum – see page 109), dominates the Strelka, flanked on the right by former warehouses and the defunct Customs House, mute witnesses to the commercial hubbub once focused here.

Menshikov's Palace, tel: 213 1112.
Tours: 10.15am–4.30pm. Closed:
Monday. Admission charge.

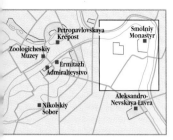

The Smolniy District

Intimately connected with the events of 1917, this peaceful residential district conceals its violent history behind the tranquil Tauride Gardens and the stunning cathedral of the Smolniy Convent. *Allow 2 hours.*

Start at metro Chernyshevskaya and turn right out of the metro and right again down Furshtadskaya Ulitsa.

1 TAVRICHESKIY SAD (Tauride Gardens)
Quiet Furshtadskaya Ulitsa leads to the gates of the Tauride Gardens, where a pensive Lenin presides over squealing children, strolling pensioners and inebriated fishermen in one of St Petersburg's most attractive parks.

2 TAVRICHESKIY DVORETS (Tauride Palace)
In the far left corner of the park stands the celebrated Tauride Palace, site of the first 'Duma' or parliament in 1906. After the Revolution, Lenin sent Red Guards in to disband the first and last sitting of the elected Constituent Assembly in 1918.

Built in 1789, the palace was a gift from Catherine the Great to her lover Prince Grigori Potemkin as a reward for the conquest of Tauris, the old name of the Crimea. In one of his frequent fits of hatred for his mother, her son Paul donated the palace to the Horse Guards for stables. (Closed to the public.)
Leave the park and go down Tavricheskaya Ulitsa towards Shpalernaya Ulitsa.

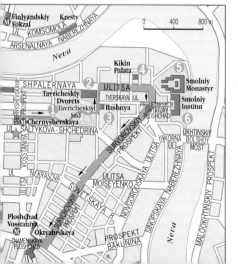

3 BASHNYA ('The Tower')
Building No 35 on the corner of Tverskaya Ulitsa is famed for its top floor apartment, dubbed 'The Tower'. It was the meeting place of one of Russia's greatest avant-garde circles, including the poets Anna Akhmatova, Alexander Blok, Osip Mandelstam and Nikolai Gumilyov. Predictably, most of them were exiled, executed or silenced by the Bolsheviks.
Head right down Shpalernaya Ulitsa.

The 18th-century Smolniy Convent, founded by Empress Elizabeth, is now an exhibition centre

4 KIKIN PALATA (Kikin's Chambers)

The view of the Smolniy Cathedral is breathtaking as you approach the convent along Shpalernaya Ulitsa, but it is worth looking at the beautifully preserved building on the left near the junction with Stavropolskaya Ulitsa. It briefly belonged to one of Peter the Great's senior bureaucrats, Alexander Kikin, before he suffered public torture and execution on Moscow's Red Square for befriending Peter's estranged son, Alexis.

5 SMOLNIY MONASTYR (Smolniy Convent)

One of St Petersburg's highlights, the icy grandeur of the Smolniy Convent is the work of the great architect Bartolomeo Rastrelli. The design, commissioned by Empress Elizabeth in 1748, originally included a vertiginous 140m belltower.

The convent's brief religious life – in 1797 it became a home for widows of the nobility – may explain the unimaginative cathedral interior. A vegetable depot during the Civil War, it now serves as an exhibition centre. You can climb up the belltower to enjoy the view over the Neva.

(The name 'Smolniy' *(smola* – tar) is derived from the shipbuilders' tar-yards on the site in Peter's time.)

6 SMOLNIY INSTITUT (The Smolniy Institute)

Adjoining the convent, the former Smolniy Institute was Russia's first school for girls, but is better known as the nerve-centre from which Trotsky and Lenin plotted the Bolshevik Revolution. As the Leningrad Party headquarters it also witnessed the murder of Party boss Sergei Kirov in 1934, marking the inception of Stalin's savage purges.

Closed to the public, the building is now the city mayor's stronghold.

Return along Survorovskiy Prospekt by trolleybus 5, 7, 11 or 16 to Ploshchad Vosstaniya metro.

Smolniy Monastyr, tel: 271 9182.
Open: 11am–5pm. Closed: Thursday.
Admission charge.

Excursions
from St Petersburg

GATCHINA

Off-limits to tourists during most of the Soviet period because of the proximity of various military bases, Gatchina is undergoing restoration to erase the scars of wartime bomb damage and official neglect. The accessible parts of Tsar Paul's family retreat give a tantalising glimpse of the unhappy 18th-century royal household.

The estate was originally a gift from Catherine the Great to her lover Count Orlov. Her son Paul took over the palace in 1783, thoroughly remodelling the building to his militaristic taste. Relations with his mother were of mutual hatred and Paul spent most of his days here or at nearby Pavlovsk (see page 128).

Only the first floor is fully restored, with the Marble Dining Room and White Hall its highlights. The ground floor exhibits the tsar's collection of armoury.

The palace grounds were designed in the fashionable English style. At dusk, the lonely pavilions and gazebos only add to the eeriness of grounds said to be haunted by ghosts of the tsar's hunting dogs.
50km south of St Petersburg. Reached by elektrichka *from Baltiyskiy Vokzal to Gatchino-Baltiyskaya station. Tel: (271) 13492. Open: 11am–5pm. Closed: Monday and last Tuesday of each month. Admission charge.*

KRONSTADT

This island naval base was scene of a sailors' uprising that rocked the infant Bolshevik government. Later it was one of Russia's key maritime installations and, as such, closed to foreigners until very recently.

Repeatedly a political barometer, the garrison at Kronstadt played a key role in the 1825 'Decembrists' uprising. Later it was instrumental in establishing Soviet power – hence the bloody ferocity with which Trotsky's Red Guards put down an insurrection by disillusioned sailors calling for an end to Bolshevik dictatorship. Over 30,000 were killed overnight on 16 March 1921.
30 minutes' hydrofoil trip from the Tuchkov Bridge on Vasilevskiy Island in summer. When the Gulf is frozen, take elektrichka *from Finlandskiy Vokzal to Gorskaya and catch a bus.*

VALAAM AND KIZHI

If you have plenty of time you could make the long excursion to the uniquely beautiful Valaam archipelago and Kizhi Peninsula. Cruises go from St Petersburg to Valaam, about 160km due north, taking at least three days for the round trip. Journeys out to Kizhi on Lake Onega, which often make a stop at Valaam, last a full five days. Bearing in mind the northern latitude, either trip is only really feasible in summer.

Valaam

Although the main attraction of the archipelago is its natural beauty, there are also a number of churches and a small working medieval monastery on the chief island, complete with carved caves where hardy monks once retreated into isolated meditation.

Kizhi

The clear northern air and austere Karelian scenery provide a perfect backdrop for one of Russia's most stunning sights: the collection of wooden architecture on Kizhi Island.

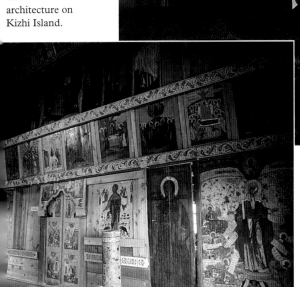

The Church of the Transfiguration, Kizhi Island and (left) some of the paintings on wood to be seen inside

How to get there

There is no shortage of tourist firms in St Petersburg advertising tours to the destinations above. The better established include: Sputnik, Ulitsa Chapygina 4. Tel: 234 3500; Nord Soyuz, Bolshaya Posadskaya Ulitsa 9a. Tel: 238 8261; and Saint Petersburg Tourist Company, Isaakievskaya Ploshchad 11. Tel: 315 5129. Camp sites are available on Valaam's islands, and hotel accommodation for Kizhi can be arranged in the mainland town of Petrozavodsk.

Intricate examples of the traditional peasant cottage, the *izba*, stand with wooden churches, the most famous of which is the astonishing Church of the Transfiguration. Bristling with 22 cupolas, it was built in 1714 entirely without nails. The island also has Russia's oldest wooden church, the tiny 1391 Church of St Lazarus, transported across Lake Onega from the Muromskiy Monastery. Unsurprisingly, Kizhi is a strictly no-smoking area!

Restore the spirits by wandering through one of the world's finest parks, at Pavlovsk

ORANIENBAUM (formerly Lomonosov)

Prince Alexander Menshikov called his estate 'Orange Tree' to draw attention to his orange plantation – its existence no mean feat given St Petersburg's climate! The Great Palace (1725) was his attempt to upstage Peter the Great's at nearby Peterhof. Its ostentatious façade, flanked by octagonal pavilions, commands a view of the Gulf of Finland. (The interior is closed for renovation.)

Beyond the lake stands a small palace built for Tsar Peter III. Nearer the Gulf in the Upper Park, the Katalnaya Gorka was an 18th-century version of the roller-coaster for aristocratic amusement. *Oranienbaum is 40km west of St Petersburg, an hour by* elektrichka *from Baltiyskiy Vokzal. Tel: 422 8806. Open: April to October only. Park open: daily 9am–10pm. All buildings closed last Monday of month; Peter's Palace closed Monday; others closed Tuesday. Admission charge.*

PAVLOVSK

Tsar Paul's estate was begun by Scottish architect Charles Cameron, whose genius for classical design is best displayed in the stunning Italian and Grecian Halls of the Grand Palace. Paul, more concerned with scale than taste, soon fired Cameron to work through every major architect of the time in his quest for splendour.

Those wearied by extravagant royal residences can wander in Pavlovsk's splendid park, Russia's largest and one of the world's best. Scattered with temples, pavilions and monuments to the lonely tsar's obsessions, the park's alleys and waterways provide endless scenic strolling (but take mosquito repellent in summer). *Pavlovsk is 30km south of St Petersburg, reached by* elektrichka *(35 minutes) from Vitebskiy Vokzal, then a 15-minute walk from the station to the Palace or catch bus 317, 370 or 383. Tel: 470 2155. Park open: daily 9am–8pm; Grand Palace open: 10am–5.30pm. Closed: Friday and first Monday of the month.*

PETRODVORETS (Peterhof)

The first of the royal pleasure palaces to be built outside St Petersburg, Petrodvorets (better known as Peterhof) is the embodiment of Peter the Great's breathtaking self-confidence. Systematically vandalised by German troops during World War II, Peterhof was almost miraculously resurrected by Soviet artisans from little more than ashes to the glorious ensemble on show today.

The Great Palace

Peterhof's finest sight is the Grand Cascade, illuminated at dusk, that sets off the façade of the Great Palace. Soon due to be reopened following an overhaul, the cascade's many sculptures and water jets are a highlight of a trip to St Petersburg.

The present palace was designed by Rastrelli, architect of the Winter Palace – Peter's original was one floor lower. The dazzling state rooms are reached by Rastrelli's Ceremonial Staircase, itself of spectacular beauty.

Monplaisir

Scene of roof-raising soirées, Monplaisir was Peter's preferred residence. More sinisterly, it was where he ruthlessly interrogated his son Alexei before ordering his execution. Outside in the garden, Peter's joke fountain, squirting the unwary who tread in front of it, reveals a childish facet of his complex personality.

Other sights

Peterhof is packed with other points of interest and it's worth joining a tour for a full excursion.

Look out for Marly Palace and Cottage Palace built for Nicholas I's family. *Peterhof is 30km west of St Petersburg, reached by hydrofoil from front of Hermitage (last boat back about 5pm), or by* elektrichka *from Baltiyskiy Vokzal to Novy Pergof and buses 351–5. Tel: 427 9527. Grounds open: daily 9am–8pm; cascade and fountains operate May to September. Closing times differ – Great Palace closed: Monday and last Tuesday of the month; Monplaisir Wednesday and last Thursday; Marly Tuesday and last Wednesday; Cottage closed Friday. Full programme at weekends only. Admission charges.*

The great Ceremonial Staircase in Peterhof

Tsarskoe Selo: the
Catherine Palace and
(below) Palace Church

furnished with semi-
precious stones).

Outside, you can
wander in the palace
gardens or row on the
ornamental ponds.

The Alexander Palace

The Alexander
Palace, retreat of the
last tsar, Nicholas II,
and built in a more
subdued neo-classical
manner, is not open, but
you can walk through the
Alexander Park behind.

Pushkin's Dacha and Lyceum

A short walk from the
Alexander Palace is the
summer house of
Alexander Pushkin, while
opposite the Catherine
Palace, on Ulitsa Komsomolskaya, you
can visit the Imperial Lyceum, where the
poet studied, its classrooms and dormitory
all preserved with period furnishings.

TSARSKOE SELO

Tsarskoe Selo ('Tsar's
Village'), with its two royal
palaces and Pushkin
connections, was renamed
Detskoe ('Children's')
Selo after 1917 when
many villas became
orphanages; from 1937
until 1992 the town was
known as Pushkin.

The Catherine Palace

Another of Rastrelli's baroque
masterpieces, the luxurious Catherine
Palace, summer residence of Empresses
Elizabeth and Catherine the Great, is
vast. Among the many resplendent
chambers is the Amber Room, originally
constructed by Rastrelli from panels
presented by Frederick of Prussia to
Peter the Great (reconstructed since as
the Nazis stole the originals).

Catherine the Great commissioned
Charles Cameron to redesign the palace
interior in 1779. His two greatest
creations are the Cameron Gallery and
the Agate Pavilion in the courtyard,

Tsarskoe Selo is 25km south of St Petersburg,
30 minutes by elektrichka *from Vitebskiy*
Vokzal to Detskoe Selo station then buses
370, 371 or 378 to the park. Catherine
Palace, tel: 465 3429. Open: 11am–5pm.
Closed: Tuesday and last Monday of the
month. Dacha, tel: 476 6990. Open:
11am–6pm. Closed: Monday, Tuesday.
Lyceum, tel: 470 7792. Open:
10.30am–4.30pm. Closed: Tuesday.
Admission charges.

GETTING AWAY FROM IT ALL

'I am as poor as nature,
As naked as the sky,
And my freedom is spectral
Like the voice of the midnight birds.'
OSIP MANDELSTAM,
1891–1938

Getting Away From it All

*E*ven the most hardened sightseer is likely to tire of the hectic pace, frantic crowds and traffic fumes of Moscow and St Petersburg. Fortunately, both cities offer a variety of means of escape; they may sometimes involve a little travelling, but the results are worth it.

MOSCOW
ARKHANGELSKOYE

Prince Golitsyn's magnificent country house is the highlight of this beautiful spot just outside the city. The house was built of stucco-covered timber by Rastrelli, architect of St Petersburg's Winter Palace, and is luxuriously appointed with tapestries and 18th-century furniture. The estate's landscaped gardens lead down to the Moskva river in a series of terraces.
Krasnogorsk Region. Tel: 561 9785. Open:

Wednesday to Sunday 11am–5pm. Admission charge. Metro: Tushinskaya, then bus 545.

BUKHTA RADOSTYEI (Bay of Joys)

Half an hour's hydrofoil (*raketa*) ride from the river boat terminal at Rechnoi Vokzal metro brings you to the 'Bay of Joys', a popular riverside picnic spot in the warmer months. Stock up with a loaf of black bread, sausage, pickled herrings, cheese and a bottle of Georgian red wine.
Phone the Moscow River Boat Company for departure and last return times. Leningradskoye Shosse 59. Tel: 457 0051. Metro: Rechnoi Vokzal.

Gorky Park, Moscow, a favourite with skaters in winter when the ponds freeze over

BOULEVARDS AND PARKS

You need not travel far to escape Moscow's urban intensity – a stroll along the ring of boulevards in the town centre is often enough to restore a little sanity. Tverskoy, Gogolevskiy and Rozhdestvenskiy Boulevards are among the best for people-watching, as old men argue over chessboards in summer and fur-coated toddlers are taken for gentle sledge rides in winter.

Alternatively, head for the forested parks on the outskirts of town. Izmailovskiy Park and Bittsa Forest are two of the best.
Metro: Izmaylovskiy Park, Bittsevskiy Park.

The ancient woodlands of Kolomenskoye, where Peter the Great played as a child

KOLOMENSKOYE

Peter the Great spent much of his childhood at this ancient and picturesque estate on the Moskva river. Originally a 14th-century village of artisans and fishermen, its commanding location made it a strategic point in Muscovy's seemingly ceaseless battles. Dmitri Donskoy massed his troops on the hill before the decisive battle of Kulikovo in 1380. Ivan the Terrible made it the first stage of his campaign to capture the Tartar stronghold of Kazan. Many of the wizened oak trees still standing were even then already several centuries old.

Today the site is an open-air museum, Muzey-Zapovednik XVI–XVII vi 'Kolomenskoye'. The rugged beauty of the 1532 Church of the Ascension is the chief attraction, closely followed by the azure cupolas of the Church of Our Lady of Kazan visible through the estate gateway. A number of unique wooden buildings were transferred to the estate in the 1930s, including the simple log cabin from which Peter directed his northern campaigns, a defence tower from the White Sea and a 17th-century mead distillery from the nearby village of Preobrazhenskoye.

A great place for sledging and cross-country skiing in winter, Kolomenskoye is at its most enchanting as the sun sets and a largely elderly congregation gathers for evening prayers at the Kazan Church.
Prospekt Andropova 39. Tel: 112 5217. Grounds open year round. Buildings open: 10am–5pm. Closed: Monday. Admission charge for the small decorative arts museum. Metro: Kolomenskaya, then follow the signs to the estate.

KUNTSEVO

The woodlands on the steep river banks between Kuntsevskaya and Bagrationovskaya metro stations are ideal for a summer picnic or for tobogganing in winter. On a clear day in autumn, the view across the river through the orange and crimson sycamore trees is stunning.
Metro: Kuntsevskaya. Exit on to Malaya Filyovskaya Ulitsa, walk 300m back towards the centre and cut up through the apartment blocks to the woodlands beyond.

A time of picturesque charm and long, cold nights; of festivities; of perilous streets and treacherous pavements ... winter is the quintessential Russian experience.

The first frosts set in at the end of *babye lyeto* – 'woman's summer' – a brief spell of warmer weather in autumn compared to the last flowering of female beauty before old age. Apart from occasional short-lived thaws, the winter in Moscow and St Petersburg lasts through to early March and the festival of Maslenitsa, its pagan origins alive in the roaring bonfires and orgiastic consumption of the soured-cream-doused pancakes – *blini* – that symbolise the sun.

On 31 December Russian children sleep restlessly in anticipation of what Ded-Moroz – 'Grandfather Frost' – and his girl helper Snegurochka will bring for Novy God – New Year – still the biggest Russian holiday.

On a more mundane level, the all-encompassing *slyakot* – a singularly Russian mixture of mud, slush and sleet that accompanies the thaw – means going out armed with a change of shoes. Everybody wears furs, but note: hell hath no fury like a cloakroom attendant who discovers your coat is missing the loop for hanging. Similarly, *babushkas* verbally lambast mothers on the street whose children they consider inadequately dressed.

RUSSIAN WINTER

Left: dressed up for the Russian winter. Above: sunbathing in the snow at the Peter-and-Paul Fortress, St Petersburg. Right: house of ice in Russia's far north

Since 988, when Prince Vladimir of Kiev rejected Islam in favour of Christianity (because the former's condemnation of alcohol was unsuitable to the Russian climate), the colder months have been the occasion for increased drinking, and each winter brings its toll of deaths by frostbite of the homeless and those who were reckless enough to stop for a snooze on the way home from a boisterous night out.

Snow and ice bring out tobogganing children, couples skating the iced paths of Gorky Park, and an army of the track-suited elderly cruising the woods on cross-country skis. Strangest of all are the ice swimmers, nicknamed *morzh* ('walruses'), whose ideal pastime in a heavy frost is to strip down and plunge into gaps in the ice before setting off on a barefooted jog across the snow.

KUSKOVO

Situated on the outskirts of Moscow, the Kuskovo estate is a wonderful escape from the city. It was built in the 18th century for Prince Sheremetev (see page 62), owner of well over a million hectares of land. Although ravaged by Napoleon's troops in 1812, a fine ensemble of Russian architecture remains, surrounded by landscaped parkland and an ornamental lake.

The two-storey wooden palace, once the scene of Sheremetev's lavish society balls, retains its opulent interior decoration and forms part of a museum of ceramics on the estate, made up of private collections nationalised after the Revolution.

The estate is also the setting for a summer season of evening concerts – check listings in the press.

Ulitsa Yunosti 2. Tel: 370 0160. Open: Tuesday to Friday 11am–7pm; weekends 10am–6pm. Admission charge. Metro: Ryazanskiy Prospekt, then bus 133.

SEREBRYANY BOR
('Silver Pine Forest')

This secluded island on the Moskva river is a favourite destination of Muscovites on hot summer weekends. Communist Party officials built the many exclusive dachas here, now being bought up by the capital's new ruling class of businessmen because of the relatively clean location upstream of heavy industry. For those not tempted to swim, the island is a great place to indulge the Russian passion for hunting mushrooms and berries.

Take trolleybus 21 from metro Polezhayevskaya along Prospekt Marshala Zhukova right on to the island.

TSARITSYNO

Surrounded by forested parks and ornamental lakes, the picturesque ruins at Tsaritsyno in the south of the city are all that remain of one of Moscow's strangest royal retreats. It was designed in red brick and limestone by Vasili Bazhenov, in a peculiar cocktail of architectural styles, for Catherine the Great. Visiting Moscow in 1787, Catherine was appalled by Tsaritsyno, reportedly describing the turret pavilions as akin to candles around a coffin. With wars against the Turks consuming ever

Moscow's beach, Serebryany Bor, a good place to relax when you need to escape from the city

A stretch of St Petersburg's Catherine Canal. The pace is slow here, and the views evocative

more of the Imperial budget, Tsaritsyno was never completed.

Restoration is under way on the park's ornamental bridges and several of the estate's buildings, including Bazhenov's Opera House. Boats can be hired on the lakes in summer.

Access to Tsaritsyno and the parks is free year round. Metro: Tsaritsyno. Leave the station from the exit nearer the front of the train, head under the railway bridges, take the right fork, turning left at the lakes to the estate entrance.

ST PETERSBURG

FINSKY ZALIV (Gulf of Finland)

If you have time to spare or a car at your disposal, you could explore the coast of the Gulf of Finland where the wealthy have their summer dachas in an area of sandy beaches and shaded woodland. Slightly inland, Lake Razliv is a favourite picnic spot near the town of Sestroretsk while heading further up the coast, you reach the village of Repino, named after the painter Ilya Repin, whose estate is now a museum.

The region is well served by elektrichka trains from Finlandskiy Vokzal (Finland Station). For the coast, pick one destined for Sestroretsk and get off at any attractive spot. Repino is reached by trains headed for Zelenogorsk. Or drive out on Primorskoe Shosse, the coastal road. Sestroretsk is 34km from the city, Repino 50km.

Repin Museum, Primorskoe Shosse 411. Open: 10am–5pm. Closed: Tuesday. Admission charge.

KANAL GRIBOYEDOVA (formerly Catherine Canal)

Without leaving the city centre, a stroll along the banks of the Catherine Canal is a good way to unwind. Starting at the Anichkov Bridge and passing the Kazan Cathedral, walk down around the back of the city centre to admire the view at St Nicholas' Cathedral before turning up the Kryukova Canal towards the Novaya Gollandiya ('New Holland') island with its abandoned warehouses and melancholy atmosphere.

In St Petersburg you can take a Neva river trip on the *Meteor* hydrofoil

(Krestovskiy Island), the biggest of the islands. *Metro: Chernaya Rechka is the nearest, followed by trams 2, 31 or 37. Yelagin Palace, tel: 239 1131. Open: Wednesday to Sunday 10am–6pm. Admission charge.*

RIVER AND CANAL RIDES

To relax, take a leisurely tour of the waterways of St Petersburg. Not only does it put a comfortable expanse of water between you and the crowds on dry land, it is also the best way to appreciate the city's architecture.

In the summer tourist season, roughly June to September, passenger cruise boats leave regularly from the Anichkov Bridge on Nevskiy Prospekt. Two options for a tour with commentary are offered: the Fontanka and Moyka canals plus the Kryukova Canal, or the Fontanka and the Neva.

Alternatively, and more expensively, you can hire a motor launch and set your own itinerary with the boatmen waiting either at the Anichkov Bridge or the Politseyskiy Bridge near the Summer Garden.

Another possibility is to take a *Meteor* or hydrofoil trip on the Neva. Boats leave for Peterhof from the mooring outside the Winter Palace or for the Gulf of Finland and Kronstadt from the Tuchkov Bridge on Vasilevskiy Island.

KIROVSKIYE OSTROVA
(Kirov Islands)

Apart from during the June White Nights, when they are the focus of much midnight revelry, the Kirov Islands on the Neva delta make for a peaceful break. Under the tsars, the rich and famous were granted permission to build summer mansions on the islands, the best of which are on Kamenniy Ostrov (Stone Island). A footbridge connects it with Yelagin Ostrov (Yelagin Island), the centrepiece of which is the Yelagin Palace, built in 1822 for Tsar Paul's widow and luxuriously preserved inside. The palace grounds make up the rest of the island. Closed to vehicles, they are known in the Soviet idiom as the Kirov Park of Culture and Rest.

The vast Primorskiy Park Pobedy (Seaside Victory Park) occupies the greater part of Krestovskiy Ostrov

DIRECTORY

'There are no roads in Russia,
only directions.'
WINSTON CHURCHILL

Shopping

*T*he appalling Soviet shopping experience is now thankfully a thing of the past – in Moscow and St Petersburg at least. Market reforms have filled the stores again and, if you have the money, you can buy just about anything you might need on your trip or as a souvenir. The same economic freedoms have also broadened the opportunities for hustlers and con-men – so make sure you get what you're paying for, especially at the souvenir markets.

Shopping in Russia
When embarking on a shopping spree, you should remember that there are broadly two kinds of shop in Russia.

The western-managed shops function just as you would expect and may accept hard currency and credit cards. Sales assistants often speak English. Even if they don't, they will be attentive and helpful.

In the ex-socialist Russian store expect to queue to see the goods, queue to pay for them and then queue to hand over the receipt and receive your purchase.

Dolls in traditional costume are an alternative to the inevitable stacking dolls

Payment is in roubles only. Although shelves are better stocked, sales assistants are still extraordinarily rude, despite a decree by the Moscow mayor in 1994 that shopkeepers are obliged to be nice to customers! Don't stand on ceremony – if you wait to be noticed, you won't leave the shop before nightfall. Lastly, don't forget to bring your own bag since few

Russian shops provide them.

Though tax-free shopping is at present limited to diplomats, this may soon change. Ask when you arrive.

Souvenirs
Amber, gold, furs, hardback art books, caviar and domestic brandies and 'champagne' are all good value in Russia. (Remember customs regulations, however – see page 180.)

The souvenirs market has exploded since the collapse of communism, resulting in a flood of ironic 'Leninist' T-shirts, Soviet-era bric-à-brac and odd items of military apparel in the tourist fleamarkets. More traditional favourites are gaudily painted mugs, plates and spoons from the village of Khokhloma outside Moscow, 'Matryoshka' stacking dolls and elaborately lacquered boxes (*palekh*). Fake versions of all these will be earnestly offered to you at the markets; to be safe, it is advisable to confine serious purchases to specialist souvenir shops where the more you pay, the better your chances of obtaining the real thing.

The Moscow haven for souvenir hunters is the Izmaylovskiy Market, open at weekends and selling everything from fighter pilots' helmets and stolen icons to handmade jewellery and traditional costumes. Bargain hard (but see **Customs**, page 180). Turn left out of metro Izmaylovskiy Park and pass the high-rise hotel complex. The market gates are in front of you.

The equivalent in St Petersburg is Klenovaya Alleya, open daily in the season. From metro Gostiniy Dvor, head towards Ploshchad Iskusstv and turn right along Inzhenernaya Ulitsa.

Both cities also have open-air art bazaars selling local contemporary work. Hard bargaining is in order here, too.

The main centre in Moscow is opposite the entrance to Gorky Park (metro Park Kultury), in St Petersburg along Nevskiy Prospekt.

Moscow's more serious souvenir shops include the Moscow Cultural Fund Salon (Pyatnitskaya Ulitsa 16, metro Novokuznetskaya) and the International Art Fund Salon (Ukrainskiy Bulvar 6, metro Kievskaya. Tel: 243 9458). A number of junk shops on the Arbat – at Nos 9, 31 and 36 – are also worth looking in.

In St Petersburg, try Naslyediye (Nevskiy Prospekt 116, metro Ploshchad Vosstaniya. Tel: 279 5067) or Russkiy Dom (Ulitsa Chaykovskovo 65, metro Chernyshevskaya. Tel: 275 1565).

Lacquered boxes, a favourite souvenir, on sale in Izmaylovskiy Market, Moscow

BOOKS
Zwemmer
Carries Moscow's biggest stock of English-language books.
Kuznetskiy Most 18. Tel: 928 2021. Metro: Kuznetskiy Most.

Bookworms in St Petersburg without a command of Russian are for the moment restricted to whatever their hotel kiosks have on offer.

CAVIAR AND 'COGNAC'
Caviar is easily available in any big food shop. It may be cheaper on the streets, but it may not be caviar – it is not unheard of for tourists to buy ball bearings in axle grease from especially enterprising salesmen.

There is plenty of caviar on offer, but make sure it is the genuine article

Locally produced drinks have all but disappeared from the streets under the deluge of imported beverages, but are nevertheless worth seeking out. Armenian '*konyak*' (brandy) is highly thought of outside the former USSR, as are Georgian and Crimean wines. Another fine souvenir is real Russian Smirnovskaya vodka, recognisable by its tapering bottle.

Try the following outlets:
Moscow:
Novoarbatsky Gastronom
Ulitsa Novy Arbat 13. Tel: 291 7685. Metro: Arbatskaya.

St Petersburg
Konyak, Shampanskoye shop
Nevskiy Prospekt 130. Tel: 277 1826. Metro: Ploshchad Aleksandra Nevskovo.

DEPARTMENT STORES
Moscow:
Gosudarstvenny Universalniy Magazin
Moscow's inimitable chief department store translates in typical Soviet style as plain State Department Store, and is better known just as GUM (pronounced 'goom'). The impressive building's vast glass canopy covers the hundreds of galleried shops within, once packed only with shoddy electrical devices, outsize brassieres and queues. Now, newly privatised, it is a mall soon to rival Paris's best. Europe's classiest boutiques and retailers are rapidly edging out the old state shops and you can buy just about anything at all.
Krasnaya Ploshchad 3. Tel: 921 5763. Metro: Ploshchad Revolyutsii.
Petrovskiy Passazh
Petrovka Ulitsa 10. Metro: Teatralnaya.

TsUM
Petrovka Ulitsa 2. Tel: 292 1157. Metro: Teatralnaya.

St Petersburg:
Gostiniy Dvor complex
Nevskiy Prospekt 36. Metro: Gostiniy Dvor.

Passazh
*Nevskiy Prospekt
48. Metro:
Gostiniy Dvor.*

FURS
A lot of furs on
sale are
Scandinavian
pelts sewn in
Turkey, so ask
carefully if you
are after the
Russian article.

A tempting display in Yeliseev's foodstore in St Petersburg's Nevskiy Prospekt

Moscow:
Arbat 28
*Ulitsa Arbat 28. Tel: 241 1081. Metro:
Arbatskaya.*
Sovmekhastoria
*Ulitsa Bolshaya Dorogomilovskaya 14. Tel:
323 4384. Metro: Kievskaya.*
    Several shops in the GUM arcade on
Red Square also sell furs.

St Petersburg:
Lena
*Nevskiy Prospekt 50. Tel: 312 4032.
Metro: Mayakovskaya.*
Mekha Rossii
*Nevskiy Prospekt 57. Metro:
Mayakovskaya.*

SPORTS SUPPLIES
Skates and skis in winter and rucksacks
etc in the summer are intermittently
available from:
In Moscow:
Olimp
*Krasnaya Presnaya Ulitsa 23. Tel: 255
9592. Metro: Krasnopresnenskaya.*

St Petersburg:
Turist
*Nevskiy Prospekt 122. Tel: 277 0279.
Metro: Ploshchad Aleksandra Nevskovo.*

SUPERMARKETS
Both cities are dotted with foreign-run
supermarkets which sell a wide range of
food, toiletries and the like, most of it
imported from western Europe. Prices are
higher than in most European countries.
Some of the larger ones are listed below.
Moscow:
Stockmann
*Zatsepskiy Val 4. Tel: 233 2602. Metro:
Paveletskaya.*
Garden Ring
*Bolshaya Sadovaya Ulitsa 5/1. Tel: 209
1572. Metro: Mayakovskaya.*
The Arbat Irish House
*Ulitsa Novy Arbat 21. Tel: 291 7641.
Metro: Arbatskaya.*
Sadko Foodland
*Bolshaya Dorogomilovskaya Ulitsa 16. Tel:
243 6659. Metro: Kievskaya.*

St Petersburg:
Babylon
*Maliy Prospekt 54, Tel: 230 8096. Metro:
Petrogradskaya.*
Spar
*Stachek Prospekt 1. Tel: 186 5177. Metro:
Narvskaya.*
Stockmann
*Finlandskiy Prospekt 1. Tel: 542 2297.
Metro Ploshchad Lenina.*

THE MARKET

The market – *rynok* – is a central element of city life in Moscow and St Petersburg. Somehow, these strongholds of small-scale capitalism managed to survive communism's assault on private property. This was not least, perhaps, because even the most dutiful party functionary relied on the markets for that little something special when the shelves of the state shops were barren of all but a few wizened beetroot and dusty jars of pickled cucumbers.

Moscow's Cheryomushinskiy or St Petersburg's Kuznechniy markets are an experience in themselves, a microcosm of the old Soviet Union. Traders from all corners of the former empire accost the casual visitor: swarthy Georgians proffer bright red roses 'for the beautiful lady, sir'; Uzbeks and Turkmen crouch over piles of watermelons and sacks of roasted sunflower seeds; buxom Ukrainians invite you to try their national favourite

Moscow's market scene: Luzhniki Stadium (top left) and Cheryomushinskiy

– huge slabs of pork fat called *salo*; fishermen from the Caspian Sea stand proudly in front of bucketfuls of red and black caviar; and old ladies in bright headscarves sell salted tomatoes and pickled garlic from their allotments in the suburbs of the city.

Some of the goods are as exotic as the salespeople, ranging from whole sturgeons and beluga whales to Armenian brandies and *kvass*, Russia's traditional black bread beer. The meat section is not for the squeamish, with cuts that have long disappeared from Western supermarkets – pig's trotters, goats' heads, complete ox tongues and internal organs best left unnamed. And, for refreshment, there is sure to be a bottle of the country's lethal moonshine, *samogon*, discreetly hidden under the counter.

The welcome is warm and the sales patter persuasive. Little has changed since the 19th century when a foreign traveller noted that the stallholders in Russia's markets have, notwithstanding their lust of gain, a cheerfulness of temperament wholly wanting to the German or the English merchant'.

Entertainment

No trip to Russia is quite complete without an evening at the legendary Bolshoy Theatre in Moscow or St Petersburg's world-famous Mariinskiy Theatre, better known by its Soviet name, the Kirov. But as befits one of the world's great cultures, entertainment possibilities are virtually endless and there is sure to be something to suit everyone. With the demise of the austere strictures of communism, nightlife is no longer limited to highbrow tastes: clubs and casinos seem to be sprouting on just about every street corner.

What's on

Planning your time amid the wealth of entertainment on offer is probably the greatest problem for culture-hungry visitors to Russia. Members of package tours may find that a trip to the Bolshoy or Mariinskiy is already included in their schedule, simplifying the decision-making process. Otherwise, the best sources of information are the various entertainments listings published in both capitals.

Most convenient are the inserts printed periodically in the English-language newspapers distributed free of charge in western-style hotels, bars and foreign-run supermarkets. The *Moscow Times* and *Moscow Tribune* publish exhaustive listings in their pages every Friday. The former also prints on the back page a short daily 'What is to be done?' column listing the evening's highlights. Similar listings are available for St Petersburg in the *Neva News* and *St Petersburg Press* newspapers.

Most hotels have a service bureau which will inform you of current events or group trips organised by local tour agencies or by the hotel itself.

Failing any of the above you will have to decipher the Russian-language posters pasted at strategic positions on the streets, hung in the windows of ticket kiosks throughout the town (see below) or advertised outside the venues concerned.

Tickets

Getting tickets is not straightforward. There are virtually no ticket agencies as such in Russia at present. In Moscow, the one dedicated location, IPC, is situated in the Metropol Hotel (1/4 Teatralniy Proezd, tel: 927 6982) and is the best bet for acquiring good seats at the Bolshoy Theatre. The service bureaux in most hotels can arrange tickets for major spectacles given sufficient warning. Neither IPC nor your hotel is likely to be able to help with minor shows and tickets at short notice. They also have the drawback of charging foreigners considerably inflated prices.

For those prepared to chance their Russian, both cities are dotted with kiosk ticket offices – *teatralnaya kassa* – which display available tickets in the window and charge at the surprisingly low local rates. Tverskaya Ulitsa in Moscow, Nevskiy Prospekt in St Petersburg and metro stations in general are where you will find the main concentrations of these. In St Petersburg you might also try the Central Ticket Office at Nevskiy Prospekt 42.

Alternatively, you can go direct to the booking office of the theatre concerned where there is also a seating plan to help

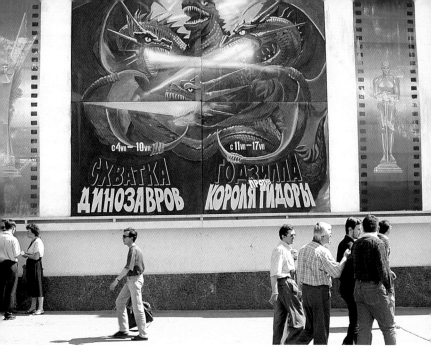

It *is* possible to see up-to-date and quality films in Russia, but cinemas showing them are few

you choose your ticket. The stalls are denoted in Russian as *amfiteatr*, *parter* or *cresla*, the dress circle as *bel-etazh*, balcony as *balkon* and a box as *lozha*.

Either way, you will be very fortunate indeed to get tickets for either the Bolshoy or Mariinskiy Theatres. If all else fails, haggle with the ticket touts who hang around the entrances well before the performance starts. Check the date and seat of the ticket – it is very easy to buy a back row seat for yesterday's show.

Most theatrical and musical performances begin at 7pm.

CINEMAS

Russians are great movie fans, but as in other parts of the world the advent of home video is slowly killing off cinema attendances. The problem is compounded by the severe financial crisis affecting domestic film studios –

output has slumped to just a handful of features a year as more and more floor space is devoted to lucrative advertisement and pop music shoots. Most cinemas now show a sorry mixture of American B-movies and 1970s European soft porn.

Nevertheless, there remain a number of first-rate cinemas showing domestic and foreign classics and hosting regular festivals devoted to great Russian directors such as Sergei Eisenstein and Andrei Tarkovsky and modern masters like Elem Klimov and Eldar Ryazanov.

Tickets are freely available in the foyers and much cheaper than in the west. Students can ask for a reduction.

Moscow:
Americom House of Cinema
Located in the Radisson Slavyanskaya Hotel, this foreigner-orientated cinema is

the place to go for the current box office hits abroad.
Berezhkovskaya Naberezhnaya 2. Tel: 941 8747. Metro: Kievskaya.

Kino Tsentr
Moscow's best cinema. Unlike most others it regularly shows foreign films with subtitles rather than a voice dub and also shows Russian classics with English subtitles.
Druzhinnikovskaya Ulitsa 15. Tel: 255 9095. Metro: Krasnopresnenskaya.

St Petersburg:
There are two cinemas comparable to Moscow's Kino Tsentr:

Dom Kino
Ulitsa Tolmacheva 1. Tel: 314 8118. Metro: Gostiniy Dvor.

Spartak
Ulitsa Saltykova-Shchedrina 8. Tel: 272 7897. Metro: Chernyshevskaya.

CLUBS AND CASINOS

Russia's *nouveaux riches* either make their money or spend it at the profusion of brand new nightclubs and casinos whose neon lights illuminate the main streets of Moscow and St Petersburg after dark. Moscow is reputedly rivalled in number of casinos only by Las Vegas!

More tasteful than their Soviet-era counterparts, they often boast fashion shows, restaurants and western DJs in addition to the dancing and gaming. They can be a little disconcerting for the uninitiated. Be prepared to be thoroughly searched for firearms by beefy guards on entry (some clubs even have special lockers for their safe keeping). Some charge a hefty entrance fee and nearly all demand a reasonable standard of dress (jacket and tie for men).

The quality and safety of any of the places mentioned below can vary drastically in a short time, largely depending on whether or not it has been adopted by one of the local mafia groups.

On leaving, you will find that taxis are a lot cheaper if you walk a few blocks away from the club entrance.

The more popular destinations in Moscow include the following:

Arlecchino
In the Kino Tsentr. Dancing and live music.
Druzhinnikovskaya Ulitsa 15. Tel: 268 8500. Metro: Krasnopresnenskaya.

Lis's
Massive disco plus casino.
Olympic Stadium, Olympiiskiy Prospekt. Tel: 288 4027. Metro: Prospekt Mira.

Manhattan Express
In the Rossiya Hotel. Excellent restaurant as well as dancing and floor shows.
Ulitsa Varvarka 6. Tel: 298 5355. Metro: Ploshchad Revolyutsii.

Metelitsa
Dancing, casino, restaurant.
Ulitsa Novy Arbat 21. Tel: 291 1130. Metro: Arbatskaya.

Night Flight
Dancing.
Tverskaya Ulitsa 17. Tel: 229 4165. Metro: Tverskaya.

Red Zone
Dancing.
TsKSA Ice Palace, Leningradskiy Prospekt 39. Tel: 213 5098. Metro: Aeroport.

Royale
Moscow's most up-market casino.
Ulitsa Begovaya 22. Tel: 945 1410. Metro: Begovaya.

St Petersburg has fewer top-quality nightspots but new ones are being advertised all the time:

Admiral

In the Hotel Astoria. Casino.
Ulitsa Bolshaya Morskaya 39.
Tel: 315 7272. Metro: Nevskiy
Prospekt.

Bamboo

In the Shanghai Restaurant.
Casino.
Sadovaya Ulitsa 12. Tel: 312
7627. Metro: Gostiniy Dvor.

Nevskiy Melody

Dancing and floor show.
Sverdlovskaya Naberezhnaya
62. Tel: 227 2676. Metro:
Novocherkasskaya.

Stardust

Dancing, casino, restaurant.
Aleksandrovskiy Park 4.
Tel: 233 2712. Metro:
Gorkovskaya.

Stiers

Dancing.
Stachek Prospekt 4. Tel: 186
5420. Metro Narvskaya.

After years of suppression,
rock is big in Russia today

Music and Theatre

You can find a world-class orchestra or ballet troupe performing on practically any day of the season (most concert halls are closed throughout July and August), and many venues host folk dance and music from all corners of the ex-USSR.

CLASSICAL MUSIC

Check in advance to find out who is playing – when the Bolshoy and Mariinskiy companies are on tour, their theatres are used by visiting companies.

Moscow concert venues
Dvorets Syezdok (Palace of Congresses)
Kreml (Trinity Gate entrance). Tel: 929 7727. Metro: Aleksandrovskiy Sad or Borovitskaya.

Moscow Conservatory
Includes two halls – *bolshoy* (large) and *maliy* (small) *zal.*
Ulitsa Bolshaya Nikitskaya 13. Tel: 229 0658. Metro: Okhotniy Ryad.

Rossiya Concert Hall
In the Rossiya Hotel complex.
Moskvoretskaya Naberezhnaya 1. Tel: 298 1124. Metro: Ploshchad Revolyutsii.

Tchaikovsky Concert Hall
Home of the State Symphony Orchestra.
4/31 Triumfalnaya Ploshchad. Tel: 299 0378. Metro: Mayakovskaya.

St Petersburg concert venues
Filarmoniya
Mikhailovskaya Ulitsa 2 for the big hall, Nevskiy Prospekt 30 for the smaller Glinka hall. Tel: 311 7333 and 312 4584 respectively. Metro: Nevskiy Prospekt.

Glinka Kapella
Often offering choral music and small ensembles.

Naberezhnaya Reki Moyki 20. Tel: 314 1153. Metro: Nevskiy Prospekt.

Oktyabrskaya Concert Hall
Ligovskiy Prospekt 6. Tel: 277 6980. Metro: Ploshchad Vosstaniya.

OPERA AND BALLET
Moscow
Bolshoy Theatre
Almost a thousand individuals make up the combined opera and ballet companies of the Bolshoy, but with dwindling state subsidies forcing ever more tours you will be lucky to catch them.
Teatralnaya Ploshchad 1. Tel: 292 0050. Metro: Teatralnaya Ploshchad.

Dvorets Syezdok (Palace of Congresses)
Home to the State Classical Ballet Theatre. See under **Classical Music** for details.

St Petersburg
Maliy Opera and Ballet Theatre
Ploshchad Iskusstv 1. Tel: 314 3758. Metro: Nevskiy Prospekt.

Mariinskiy Theatre
As with Moscow's Bolshoy company financial constraints make it tricky to catch the house company in action.
Teatralnaya Ploshchad 2. Tel: 114 5424. Metro: Sadovaya.

JAZZ, ROCK AND POP
Russia today has a vibrant rock and jazz scene, and both cities offer the full range, from smoke-filled jazz clubs and underground hard rock dens to full-scale concerts. Ever more foreign stars are including Russia on their European tours; the English-language press carries

announcements well in advance.

Phone ahead for current opening times (usually Friday and weekend evenings) or see press for concert details.

Moscow's favourite venues include:

Arbat Blues Club
Aksakov Pereulok 11.
Tel: 291 1546. Metro:
Arbatskaya.

Arkadia Jazz Club
Teatralniy Proezd 3.
Tel: 926 9008. Metro: Teatralnaya.

The Bunker Club
Rock and pop.
Trifonovskaya Ulitsa 56. Tel: 284 5834.
Metro: Rizhskaya.

Sexton FOZD Club
Heavy rock, punk, garage.
Pervy Baltiyskiy Pereulok 6/21. Tel: 151
121. Metro: Sokol.

Tabula Rasa
Everything from folk to 'performance art'.
Luzhnetskaya Naberezhnaya 2/4. Tel: 244
9474. Metro: Sportivnaya.

St Petersburg's better known locations include:

Art Club Café
All sorts.
Kanal Griboyedova 3. Tel: 314 5273.
Metro: Nevskiy Prospekt.

Jazz Hall.
Zagorodniy Prospekt 27. Tel: 164 8565.
Metro: Vladimirskaya.

Okoshka
Jazz.
Ulitsa Bolshaya Morskaya 58. No phone.
Metro: Nevskiy Prospekt.

Tamtam Club
Hard rock and punk.
Bolshoy Prospekt 46.
No phone. Metro:
Vasileostrovskaya.

THEATRE

A command of Russian is essential for full enjoyment of theatre performances.

Moscow's more important theatres include:

Chekhov Moscow Art Theatre
Kamergerskiy Pereulok 3. Tel: 229 8760.
Metro: Teatralnaya Ploshchad.

Estrada Theatre
Bersenevskaya Naberezhnaya 20/2. Tel:
230 0444. Metro: Borovitskaya.

Maliy Theatre
Teatralnaya Ploshchad 1/6. Tel: 923 2621.
Metro: Teatralnaya Ploshchad.

Lenkom Theatre
Ulitsa Chekhova 6. Tel: 299 9668. Metro:
Pushkinskaya.

Russian Army Theatre
Suvorovskaya Ploshchad 2. Tel: 281 5120.
Metro: Novoslobodskaya.

Taganka Theatre
Taganskaya Ploshchad. Tel: 272 6300.
Metro: Taganskaya.

St Petersburg:

Bolshoy Drama Theatre.
Reki Fontanki Naberezhnaya 65. Tel: 310
9242. Metro: Sennaya Ploshchad.

Maliy Drama Theatre
Ulitsa Rubinshteina 18. Tel: 113 2028.
Metro: Vladimirskaya.

Pushkin Drama Theatre
Aleksandrinskaya Ploshchad 2. Tel: 311
6139. Metro: Gostiniy Dvor.

THE BOLSHOY

The origins of Moscow's greatest ballet and opera company, the Bolshoy, date back to 1776 when the Moscow procurator, Prince Urusov, formed the first permanent Russian theatre company from the serfs on his estate. They performed in the mansion of his friend Count Vorontsov before the company was established, four years later, as the Petrovskiy Theatre on the site at the end of Ulitsa Petrovka where it remains today.

The monumental classical building that dominates Teatralnaya Ploshchad

Many great Russian works, most famously Tchaikovsky's ballet *Swan Lake*, were premiered at the Bolshoy, but it was not until Soviet times, with Moscow again the capital, that it emerged from the shadow of St Petersburg's Mariinskiy Theatre, better known as the Kirov. During the Bolshoy's heyday in the 1960s and 1970s, opera houses around the world

is the third Bolshoy Theatre. The first burned down in 1805 as did its successor in 1853. The final version outdoes London's Covent Garden and Milan's La Scala in sheer scale, and is celebrated for its superb acoustics: as the architect remarked: 'It is built like a musical instrument.'

were packed with audiences mesmerised by the company's performances of Stravinsky's *Petrushka* and Khachaturian's *Gayane* with its breathtaking 'Sabre Dance'.

Those days are over. The Bolshoy's repertoire has been cut along with once lavish state subsidies, and top dancers

The great Bolshoy Theatre (left and below) dates from the mid-19th century; the company (in *Giselle*, far left) goes back to the 18th century

are loaned abroad to raise much-needed funds. Each season is punctuated by pay disputes and strikes by the company's 900 members. A long-standing feud was brought to a head in 1995 when the much-loved artistic director resigned after a battle with theatre authorities; the dancers promptly walked out of a performance in protest. When they appeared in court a few days later, the capital was left to wonder whether the flagship of Russia's 200-year-old ballet tradition would survive into the 21st century.

National Holidays and Festivals

*T*oday new holidays marking turning-points in the struggle against Soviet power take their place alongside resurrected religious festivals in the Orthodox calendar. Landmarks in Bolshevik history that were once solemnly celebrated are now low-key events. Both Moscow and St Petersburg host a series of annual arts and music festivals.

Traditional costumes worn during the Russian Winter festival

7 January: **Orthodox Christmas**, with all-night liturgies in church.

13/14 January: **Orthodox New Year** – not officially a holiday but treated as such.

27 January: **Breaking of the Siege of Leningrad**. A public holiday in St Petersburg.

FEBRUARY/MARCH

23 February: **Defenders of the Fatherland Day**. The successor of Red Army Day, no longer a national holiday, but still the occasion of public drinking parties.

February/March: **Maslenitsa**, marking the end of winter and the beginning of Lent. Not a public holiday but celebrated by huge feasting (see page 134).

DECEMBER/JANUARY

25 December–5 January: **Russian Winter** festival. A secular celebration with family parties and cultural programmes at the two cities' main venues (see pages 150–1). **New Year's Day** (1 January) is Russia's foremost holiday, with present-giving by Ded-Moroz, 'Grandfather Frost' (see page 134).

19 February–5 March: **Farewell to Russian Winter** festival in St Petersburg. Sleigh rides and traditional food, costumes and dancing, based at the Olgino campsite (*18km along Primorskoe Shosse. Tel: 238 3552*).

8 March: **International Women's Day**. A day off for everybody except city flower-sellers.

Victory Day: parade of
ex-servicemen

MARCH/APRIL
Easter, *paskh*a, is
the chief Orthodox
festival. Children
colour eggs and
enjoy the traditional
dish of sweetened
curds with raisins, also called *paskha*.

APRIL/MAY
End of April/early May: **Musical Spring**
festival in St Petersburg. International
concerts at the city's main venues (see
pages 150–1).

MAY/JUNE
1/2 May: **International Working
People's Solidarity Day**. A day for
demonstrations by communists and a
holiday for everyone else.
9 May: **Victory Day**. Celebrates the end
of the Soviet Union's participation in
World War II. Parades and wreath-laying
in Moscow's Park Pobedi and at the
Tomb of the Unknown Soldier and
processions of veterans along Nevskiy
Prospekt in St Petersburg.
12 June: **Russian Independence Day**.
Commemorates Russia's secession from
the Soviet Union in 1991.

JUNE/JULY
21 June–1 July: **White Nights** festival in
St Petersburg. Long nights celebrating the
summer solstice when the sun virtually
never sets. Informal partying on the
streets, plus concerts on Yelagin Island
(*metro Chernaya Rechka, then overland
transport heading down Primorskiy Prospekt
to the bridge*). Crowds gather on the river
embankment to watch the bridges being
raised just after 1.30am.

AUGUST/SEPTEMBER
First four days of August: **Love Street
Festival** in Moscow. Off-beat street
entertainments and fringe art around
Pokrovskiy Bulvar (*metro: Chistiye Prudy*)
and in Moscow's clubs (see page 148).
21 August: **Anniversary of 1991 Putsch**.
Marks the failure of the coup leaders to
oust Gorbachev and save the Soviet
Union.
8 September: **Siege of Leningrad Day**.
Not a public holiday, but a day of
mourning and remembrance in St
Petersburg.

OCTOBER/NOVEMBER
7 October: **Constitution Day**.
Established to recognise Brezhnev's 1977
Constitution (may soon lapse).
7/8 November (25/26 October by old
Russian calendar): **Revolution Day**.
Once celebrated by the Soviet arsenal
rolling across Red Square and now
marked by communist marches.
Mid-November: **Autumn Rhythms** jazz
festival in St Petersburg, centred on the
city's jazz clubs (see page 151).
Autumn (odd years only): **Moscow Film
Festival** (see English-language press for
details).

DECEMBER
12 December: **Constitution Day**. This
one celebrates the new constitution
adopted in 1993.

Children

Snow-storms and sledging make the Russian winter fun for children of all ages, but even in the summer months Moscow and St Petersburg have plenty to keep youngsters interested.

Delphinari (Dolphinarium)
In Moscow's Palace of Water Sports (Dvorets Vodnovo Sporta), dolphins, seals and a beluga whale called Yegor are guaranteed to delight on a rainy day. *Ulitsa Mironovskaya 27. Tel: 369 7966. Shows: Wednesday, Thursday, Friday 3pm, 7pm; Saturday, Sunday 11am, 1pm, 4pm, 6pm. Admission charge. Metro: Semyonovskaya, Izmaylovskiy Park.*

Museums
Those in Moscow likely to appeal to youngsters include the Borodino Battle Panorama and the Space Travel, Armed Forces and Polytechnical museums (see pages 56–8).

Life-size effigies of Russia's good, bad and ugly in Moscow's waxworks exhibition appeal to children of all ages. *Tverskaya Ulitsa 14. Tel: 229 8552. Open: 11am–7pm. Closed: Monday. Metro: Mayakovskaya.*

In St Petersburg, the dungeons of the Peter-Paul Fortress (see pages 110–1) and Peter the Great's extraordinary Kunstkammer (Museum of Anthropology and Ethnography – see page 108) will capture any teenager's imagination. The Historical Waxworks, Ethnography and Naval museums (see pages 108–9), as well as the *Aurora* Cruiser (see pages 90–1), may also prove popular.

Parks
Russian amusement parks have a long way to go if they want to rival Euro-

Disney but what they lack in hi-tech rides is made up for by the holiday atmosphere and low fares.

Park im A M Gorkovo (Gorky Park) in the centre of Moscow boasts a roller-coaster, boating lake and magnificent Ferris wheel. *Krymskiy Val Ulitsa 9. Tel: 237 0707. Metro: Park Kultury.*

Much the same on a less grand scale is on offer in St Petersburg's Tauride Gardens (see page 124) and **Kirov Park** (*Yelagin Ostrov 4. Tel: 239 0911. Metro: Chernaya Rechka then tram 2, 31, 37*).

Youngsters fascinated by things military will enjoy the collection of World War II hardware in Moscow's **Park Pobedy** (Victory Park). *Kutuzovskiy Prospekt. Tel: 148 5550. Metro: Kutuzovskaya.*

River rides
A cruise in a motor launch among the canals of St Petersburg restores the culture-sated, young or old (see page 138). Hydrofoil and pleasure boat trips tour the Moscow river in warmer months. You can board at several locations, but the most convenient are next to Kievskaya Vokzal (Kievskiy railway station) and on the embankment at Gorky Park.

Theatre and Circus
Puppet theatres are a well-loved Russian tradition and even though the shows are in Russian, smaller children will be fascinated.

All the fun of the fair in Moscow's Gorky Park

Moscow:
Obraztsova Puppet Theatre
Sadovaya-Samotyochnaya Ulitsa 3. Tel: 299 3310. Metro: Tsvetnoy Bulvar.
St Petersburg:
Bolshoy Puppet Theatre
Ulitsa Nekrasova 10. Tel: 273 6672. Metro: Mayakovskaya.
Sharmanka
Moskovskiy Prospekt 151a. Tel: 294 6311. Metro: Park Pobedy.

No trip to Russia is complete without a visit to the circus. The shows are spectacular, with dancing bears, Cossack acrobats and the world's best clowns.
Moscow:
New Circus
Prospekt Vernadskovo 7. Tel: 930 2815. Metro: Universitet.
Old Circus
Tsvetnoy Bulvar 13. Tel: 200 6889. Metro: Tsvetnoy Bulvar.
St Petersburg:
Ploshchad Belinskovo 1. Tel: 210 4411. Metro: Nevskiy Prospekt, Gostiniy Dvor.

Views of the city
The roof-top panoramas from the Ostankino TV tower in Moscow and from St Isaac's Cathedral in St Petersburg are breathtaking (see pages 63 and 102 respectively).

Zoos
Moscow and St Petersburg zoos must rank as two of the least attractive animal sanctuaries in the world. Nevertheless, most children are likely to spend a perfectly happy summer's afternoon wandering among the polar bears and popcorn sellers.
Muscovskiy Zoopark (Moscow Zoo)
Bolshaya Gruzinskaya Ulitsa 1. Tel: 252 3580. Open: 9am–8pm summer, 9am–5pm winter. Admission charge. Metro: Barrikadnaya, Krasnopresnenskaya.
Zoopark (St Petersburg Zoo)
Aleksandrovskiy Park 1. Tel: 232 2839. Open: 10am–8pm. Admission charge. Metro: Gorkovskaya.

Sport

*A*s one of the world's greatest sporting nations, Russia has a lot to offer sports fans of almost every persuasion. You can enjoy first-rate football and ice hockey matches for a fraction of the cost at home, and there is ample opportunity to get involved yourself – from skiing and skating to hunting wild boar or flying a Soviet jet! And at the end of the day, you can treat yourself to a Russian steam bath.

It's men only in this pool in the Krasnopresnenskiy Baths, Moscow

BATHHOUSES

Getting steamed up at the *banya* is not so much a way of getting clean as a whole Russian sub-culture in itself. *Cognoscenti* of the *banya* don't expect to spend less than three hours relaxing in the hot and cold rooms, playing pool, working out, philosophising and drinking beer – all, of course, completely nude.

Remember to take your own towel, toiletries and sandals. Birch twig *veniki*, for mutual exfoliation, are sold on the premises. Sexes strictly segregated.

Moscow:

Sandunovskiye Banyi

The best *banya* by far, their elegant décor making them a sight in themselves. *Neglinnaya Pereulok 14. Tel: 925 4631. Metro: Kuznetskiy Most.*

St Petersburg:

Nevskaya Banya

Ulitsa Marata 5–7. Tel: 312 1379. Metro: Mayakovskaya.

BOWLING ALLEYS

Moscow:

Kosmos Hotel

In the hotel basement.

Prospekt Mira 150, Tel: 217 0786. Metro: VDHKh.

St Petersburg:

Hotel Pribaltiskaya

Korablestroiteley Ulitsa 14. Tel: 356 0263. Metro: Primorskaya.

CROSS-COUNTRY SKIING

Flat terrain rules out downhill skiing but the cross-country variety is hugely popular. Head for any of the outlying parks in winter. Skis can be very cheaply acquired at most sports shops (see page 143).

FLYING AND BALLOONING

BSC (tel: 238 4511) organise helicopter rides over St Petersburg; tour operators **Podmoskovye** (tel: 975 9545) offer the same over Moscow.

In St Petersburg, contact **Aerotur** (tel: 264 5018) for hot-air balloon tours of the city and light aircraft flights.

The ultimate flying experience must be getting behind the controls of a Soviet MiG 29 fighter and taking it for a spin.

MiGs Etc in Tampa, USA organise full training courses at Moscow's Zhukovskiy Airfield and also offer T72 tank driving in St Petersburg. Tel: (001) 813 923 0607.

GOLF
Popular with Moscow's image-conscious *nouveaux riches*, the up-market **Tumba Golf Club** also accepts green fees.
Ulitsa Dovzhenko 1. Tel: 147 6254. Metro: Universitet, then bus 67 to Ulitsa Mosfilmovskaya.

HORSE RACING
Risk a few roubles on fast action buggy racing in the centre of Moscow on Wednesdays and weekends at the **Hippodrome**, *Ulitsa Begovaya 22. Tel: 945 4516. Metro: Begovaya.*
The **Metellitsa complex** has betting facilities and satellite coverage of British horse and greyhound meetings.
Ulitsa Novy Arbat 21. Tel: 291 1130. Metro: Arbatskaya.

HORSERIDING
It's hard to beat the romance of riding through birch forests in springtime or taking a horse-drawn sleigh ride after a fresh snowfall.
Moscow:
For forest pony trekking, contact the **Ulan Riding Club**, *Ulitsa Verkhnaya 5. Tel: 976 0882. Metro: Petrovsko-Razumovskaya.*
St Petersburg:
Prostor Park stables organise pony riding and sleigh rides.

Krestovskiy Prospekt 22. Tel: 230 7873. Metro: Gorkovskaya, then tram 34.

HUNTING
The 55,000-hectare **Ozerinskoe Reserve** outside Moscow was Brezhnev's favourite hunting ground. A well-kept lodge includes a restaurant which will roast the results of the day's sport in the evening.
Contact the **Moscow Tour Club** (tel: 203 4820, 202 2291).

ICE HOCKEY
When it's too cold for football, passions switch to ice hockey, played at world standard in Russia's two big cities. International matches are advertised in the local press. Tickets at stadiums.
In Moscow:
Moscow's soccer teams (see page 160) all have corresponding hockey squads, of which the CSKA Penguins are the best.
St Petersburg:
See excellent SKA St Petersburg at the **Yubileiniy Stadium**
Prospekt Dobrolyubova 19. Tel: 238 4122. Metro: Petrogradskaya.

Cross-country ski racing, a popular pastime

ICE SKATING

You can skate the icy boulevards of Moscow's Gorky Park in winter or visit one of many covered rinks. Some places hire out skates but bring extra pairs of socks in case your size isn't available.

Moscow:

Gorky Park

The rink turns into a disco on ice in the evenings. Skate hire available.
Krymskiy Val Ulitsa 9. Tel: 237 0707. Metro: Park Kultury.

Northern Lights rink

At the Luzhniki Sports Complex. Skate hire available.
Luzhnetskaya Naberezhnaya 24. Tel: 246 5515. Metro: Sportivnaya.

St Petersburg:

The **Tauride Gardens** provide a picturesque skating venue.
Ulitsa Saltykova-Shchedrina 50. Tel: 272 6044. Metro: Chernyshevskaya.

Yubileiniy Palace of Sports

Skate hire available.
Prospekt Dobrolyubova 19. Tel: 238 4061. Metro: Vasileostrovskaya, then tram 18, 37.

JOGGING

Moscow's expatriate community gathers at 2pm outside the Ukraine Hotel on Sundays all year round for the Hash House Harriers' run around the city. Lighthearted fun with ritual beer drinking at the end. Contact your embassy for details.
Kutuzovskiy Prospekt 2/1. Metro: Kievskaya.

SAILING

The following centres offer leisure yachting in the summer months but call ahead to confirm availability.

Moscow:

Spartak Yacht Club charters yachts and instructors on an hourly rate and can arrange longer trips to St Petersburg or Astrakhan on the Volga delta.
Dolgoprudniy Town, Naberezhnaya Ulitsa 4a. Tel: 408 2500, 576 0202. 5km along Dimitrovskoe Shosse or by elektrichka from Savyolovskiy Vokzal.

St Petersburg:

The Baltic Shipping Company Yacht Club organises sailing in the Gulf of Finland and can also supply motorboats.
Naberezhnaya Martynova 92, Krestovskiy Island. Tel: 230 7585, 235 1945. Metro: Gorkovskaya, then tram 26 to terminal.

SOCCER

Russians adore soccer, and do so with a refreshing lack of European-style hooliganism. Tickets are always available for local matches on the day at the stadium. The season is from March to October.

Moscow:

Moscow's chief soccer teams, Spartak, Dinamo and CSKA, play respectively at:

Sportivnaya Arena Luzhniki (Luzhniki Stadium)
Luzhnetskaya Naberezhnaya 24. Tel: 246 5518. Metro: Sportivnaya.

Stadion Dinamo (Dinamo Stadium)
Leningradskiy Prospekt 36. Tel: 212 7092, Metro: Dinamo.

Stadion CSKA
Leningradskiy Prospekt 39a. Tel: 213 2288. Metro: Aeroport.

St Petersburg:

Zenit Leningrad plays at **Stadion Kirova** (Kirov Stadium) on Krestovskiy Island.
Morskoy Prospekt 1. Tel: 235 0078. Metro: Petrogradskaya, then bus 71A to terminal.

SWIMMING

Many hotels have swimming pools on the premises. If yours doesn't, try the following.

Sign outside the Dinamo sports club in St Petersburg

Moscow:
Olympic Penta Hotel
Olympiyskiy Prospekt 18/1. Tel: 288 1333. Metro: Prospekt Mira.
Radisson Slavyanskaya Hotel
Berezhkovskaya Naberezhnaya 2. Tel: 941 8027. Metro: Kievskaya.
St Petersburg:
Pribaltiyskaya Hotel
Korablestroiteley Ulitsa 14. Tel: 356 0263. Metro: Primorskaya.
St Petersburg Hotel
Vyborgskaya Naberezhnaya 5. Tel: 542 9123. Metro: Ploshchad Lenina.

TENNIS

Tennis is a boom sport in Russia and the country's best compete against foreign stars in Moscow's Kremlin Cup, held each autumn. See local press for details. You can also have a few sets yourself at the following venues.

Moscow:
Chaika Tennis Courts
Turchaninov Pereulok 1/3. Tel: 246 1344. Metro: Park Kultury.
Petrovskiy Park Tennis Club
Leningradskiy Prospekt 36. Tel: 212 8351. Metro: Dinamo.
St Petersburg:
The Tennis Club
Konstantinovskiy Proezd 23. Tel: 235 0407. Tram 26 from metro Gorkovskaya.

WORKOUT

Both Moscow and St Petersburg have good selections of well-equipped gyms, including the following venues:

Moscow:
Chaika Sport Complex
Turchaninov Pereulok 1/3. Tel: 246 1344. Metro: Park Kultury.
Olympic Penta Hotel
Olympiyskiy Prospekt 18/1. Tel: 971 6101. Metro: Prospekt Mira.
St Petersburg:
Hokuto
Inzhenernaya Ulitsa 13, 3rd floor. Tel: 113 7228. Metro: Gostiniy Dvor.
World Class Gym
Kamenoostrovskiy Prospekt 26/28. Tel: 232 7581. Metro: Gorkovskaya. Also in Grand Hotel Europe, Mikhaylovskaya Ulitsa 1/7. Tel: 119 6000.

Food and Drink

*A*s market reforms start to bite, Russia is rapidly overcoming its once well-deserved reputation as a gastronomic disaster area. In Moscow and St Petersburg at least, the days of barely edible food and appalling service are all but a distant memory and the hungry traveller can look forward to a top-class introduction to one of the world's most underrated cuisines.

Eating habits
The economic strife in the wake of the Soviet system's collapse means that most Russians are less concerned with *what* they eat than with getting enough of it. Many are struggling to maintain any eating habit at all. Consequently, tourists should bear in mind that they are in a somewhat artificial position. Although Caspian caviar and Siberian salmon are indeed key elements of the traditional menu, most citizens get by on large quantities of bread, potatoes and cabbage.

The Russian breakfast is generally a light affair centred on a good deal of strong, black tea, cold meat and cheese. It is often accompanied by *kefir*, a yoghurt-like drink much praised for its stomach-settling qualities the morning after the night before. Hotel breakfasts may add extra delicacies such as *blini* (pancakes) with honey.

Soups are very much a lunchtime dish, served piping hot and with a generous spoonful of soured cream stirred in. *Pirozhki* (savoury doughnuts), a variation on ravioli called *pelmyeni* and the southern favourite of *shashlyk* – meat kebabs – are also midday staples, often served up with boiled buckwheat or a mayonnaise-doused salad. A slice of black bread, as with any meal, is always on offer.

Dinner is easily the most elaborate meal and, if eating out, Russians like to make an occasion of it. Hot and cold *zakuski* (hors d'oeuvre) – typically smoked fish, wild mushrooms, hams and *blini* with red or black caviar – are almost enough in themselves, but Russians spread the load by dancing, philosophical debate and loquacious toasting throughout the evening. Traditionally, there is little concept of a quiet night out for two!

Drinking
Deeply ingrained in the culture despite occasional efforts to eradicate it, drinking on a grand scale is a national tradition and is

Living it up Russian style – *blini* (pancakes) with caviar

Centrepiece of the Russian tea table: the samovar

focused firmly on the vodka bottle. Vodka (see pages 170–1) is drunk neat in shots, preferably chilled, and followed up with a bite of marinaded fish or pickled cucumber. Be warned – Russian tolerance of vodka is famously higher than that of most tourists. One or two toasts are unavoidable but then exercise a little caution, remembering that vodka-induced drunkenness steals up extremely rapidly.

The other great Russian love is tea. Drunk in copious quantities and without milk, tea is often served with a side saucer of homemade jam in place of sugar. Coffee is also highly prized, usually presented Turkish-style and heavily sweetened unless you specify otherwise (*byez sakhara* – without sugar).

Table etiquette

A meal out in Russia involves a greater emphasis on etiquette than in the west, with men expected to seat their partners and administer all drinks. (Single women should never be seated at the table corner – as any *babushka* will tell you, this means they will not marry for seven years!)

It's bad luck to leave empty bottles on the table, bad form not to finish opened ones and a round of drinks should always be preceded by a toast. Toasts to health (*vashye zdorovye!*) require you to down your glassful in one. Smoking is acceptable at all junctures of the evening and non-smoking areas in restaurants are rare indeed.

If invited back home to eat, you ought to bring along a contribution to the meal (chocolates or a bottle of something) and flowers for your hostess.

Menu Guide

MEALS
ЗАВТРАК – *zah*vtrak – **breakfast**
ОБЕД – a*byed* – **lunch**
УЖИН – *oo*zhin – **dinner**
ЗАКУСКИ – za*koo*ski – **starters/
appetisers**
САЛАТ – sa*laht* – **salad**
СУП – soop – **soup**
ПЕРВЫЕ БЛЮДА – p*yer*viye b*lyoo*da –
first course, usually soup
ВТОРЫЕ БЛЮДА – vtor*ee*ye
b*lyoo*da/gar*yahch*i b*lyoo*da – **second or
'hot' course**
ДЕСЕРТ – de*syert* – **dessert**
ФРУКТЫ – *frook*ti – **fruit**

MEAT AND FISH
МЯСО – *myas*a – **meat**
ГОВЯДИНА – gav*yahd*ina – **beef**
СВИНИНА – svin*een*a – **pork**
БАРАНИНА – ba*rahn*ina – **lamb/mutton**
ТЕЛЯТИНА – tel*yaht*ina – **veal**
КУРИЦА – *koor*itsa – **chicken**
КОЛБАСА – kolba*sah* – **sausage**
РЫБА– *ri*ba – **fish**
ЛОСОСЬ / ГОРБУША / СЁМГА –
lasos/gar*boosh*a/*syom*ga – **salmon**
ТРЕСКА – tres*ka* – **cod**
ФОРЕЛЬ – far*yel* – **trout**
ОСЕТРИНА /СЕВРЮГА – ase*treen*a/
se*vry*ooga – **sturgeon**
ЧЁРНАЯ / КРАСНАЯ ИКРА –
*chyor*naya/*kras*naya i*krah* – **black/red
caviar**

VEGETABLES, FRUIT AND OTHER FOODS
МОРКОВЬ– mar*kohv* – **carrots**
СВЁКЛА – s*vyok*la – **beetroot**
КАПУСТА – ka*poos*ta – **cabbage**
КАРТОФЕЛЬ – kar*tof*el – **potatoes**
ЛУК - look – **onion**

ОГУРЦЫ – agoort*si* – **cucumber**
ПОМИДОЫ – pomi*dor*i – **tomatoes**
ЯБЛОКО – *yah*bloka – **apple**
АПЕЛЬСИН – apel*seen* – **orange**
ДЫНЯ – *deen*ya – **melon**
БАНАН – ba*nahn* – **banana**
ЯЙЦА – *yait*sa – **eggs**
РИС – rees – **rice**
ХЛЕБ – khl*yeb* – **bread**
МОРОЖЕНОЕ – ma*rozh*noye – **ice-crea▮**
ТОРТ – tort – **cake, gâteau**

COOKING METHODS
КОПЧЕННЫЙ – kap*chyon*y – **smoked**
ВАРЁННЫЙ – var*yon*y – **boiled**
ЖАРЕННЫЙ – *zhar*eny – **fried**
ПЕЧЁННЫЙ – pe*chyon*y – **baked**
СОЛЁННЫЙ – sal*yon*y – **salted**

TRADITIONAL DISHES
ВИНЕГРЕТ – vin*ye*gr*yet* – **diced vegetab▮
salad**
САЛАТ ОЛИВЬЕ / СТОЛИЧНЫЙ САЛА▮
– sal*aht* oli*vyeh*, sto*leech*ny sal*aht* – **diced
meat, potatoes, and vegetables in
mayonnaise or soured cream**
БОРЩ – borshch – **beetroot soup**
ЩИ – shchi – **cabbage soup**
УХА – oo*kha* – **fish soup**
ХАРЧО – khar*cho* – **spicy Caucasian
mutton soup**
СОЛЯНКА – sal*yahn*ka – **thick fish or
meat soup with potatoes**
ОКРОШКА – a*krosh*ka – **cold soup mad▮
from salad, cold meat and *kvas***
ГРИБЫ – gri*bi* – **mushrooms, often
marinaded or baked in soured crea▮**
БЛИНЫ – bli*ni* – **small pancakes,
traditionally served with soured
cream and caviar**
ПЕЛЬМЕНИ – pel*myen*i – **a heavy versi▮
of ravioli served in soured cream**

ПИРОЖКИ – pirazh*ki* – **pies of meat, cabbage, etc in fried dough**
БЕФСТРОГАНОВ – byef*stroh*ganov – **beef stroganoff, strips of beef in sour cream sauce**
КОТЛЕТЫ ПО КИЕВСКИЙ – kaht*lyeht*i pa *kee*yevsky – **chicken Kiev**
КУЛИБЯКА – kooli*byah*ka – **generally fish, especially salmon, *en croûte***
ГОЛУБЦЫ – golubt*si* – **cabbage leaves stuffed with meat and rice**
ЖАРКОЕ – *zhar*koye – **spicy meat casserole in earthenware pot**
ШАШЛЫК – shash*leek* – **kebabed meat**
ХАЧАПУРИ – khacha*poor*i – **Caucasian flat bread stuffed with cheese**

SAUCES AND CONDIMENTS
СМЕТАНА – sme*tahn*a – **soured cream**
МАЙОНЕЗ – maiyone*hz* – **mayonnaise**
ТОМсТНЫЙ СОУС – to*maht*ny sohs – **tomato sauce**
СЛИВОЧНОЕ МАСЛО – *sleev*ochnoye *mah*sla – **butter**
СОЛЬ – sohl – **salt**
ПЕРЕЦ – *pyer*ets – **pepper**
ГОРЧИЦА – gar*cheet*sa – **mustard**
САХАР – *sakh*ar – **sugar**

DRINKS
ВОДА – va*dah* – **water**
МИНЕРАЛЬНАЯ ВОДА – miner*ahl*naya va*dah* s*gahz*om/byez *gahz*a – **mineral water carbonated/still**
СОК – sok – **fruit juice**
БЕЛОЕ / КРАСНОЕ ВИНО – byel*oye*/*kras*noye vi*noh* – **white/red wine**
СЛАДКОЕ / СУХОЕ – *slad*koye/su*khoye* – **sweet/dry**
ВОДКА – *vod*ka – **vodka**
КОНЬЯК – kon*yahk* – **brandy**
ПИВО – *pee*va – **beer**
ШАМПАНСКОЕ – sham*pahn*skoye – **'champagne' (Russian sparkling wine)**

ЛИКЁРЫ – liky*or*i – **liqueurs**
ЧАЙ (С МОЛОКОМ / С ЛИМОНОМ / С САХАРОМ / БЕЗ САХАРА) – chai (smala*kom* / sli*moh*nom / *sakh*arom / byez *sakh*ara) – **tea (with milk, lemon, sugar, without sugar)**
КОФЕ (С САХАРОМ / БЕЗ САХАРА) – *koh*fee (*sakh*arom / byez *sakh*ara) – **coffee (with/without sugar)**

USEFUL WORDS AND PHRASES
РЕСТОРАН – resta*rahn* – **restaurant**
КАФЕ – ka*feh* – **café**
БАР – bar – **bar**
КУРЯЩИЕ ИЛИ НЕКУРЯЩИЕ МЕСТА? – koor*yashi* ili *nye*kooryashi myest*ah*? – **Smoking or non-smoking places?**
МЕНЮ – men*yoo* – **menu**
ОФИЦИАНТ – afit*syant* – **waiter**
СТАКАН – sta*kahn* – **glass (tumbler)**
БОКАЛ – ba*kahl* – **glass (wine glass)**
ЧАЩКА – *chash*ka – **cup**
ТАРЕЛКА – tar*yel*ka – **plate**
НОЖ – nozh – **knife**
ВИЛКА – *veel*ka – **fork**
ЛОЖКА – *lozh*ka – **spoon**
ТУАЛЕТ – tooah*lyet* – **washroom**
ПЕПЕЛЬНИЦА – *pye*pelneetsa – **ashtray**
ЧТО ВЫ РЕКОМЕНДУИТЕ? – shtoh vwi rekomen*doo*eetyeh? – **What do you recommend?**
МОЖНО ЕЩЁ…? – *mozh*na ye*shyoh* …? – **May I have some more …?**
ПРИЯТНОГО АППЕТИТА – pri*yaht*nava ape*teet*a – **Bon appétit**
ОЧЕНЬ ВКУСНО – *oh*chyen vkoos*na* – **Very tasty**
ЭТО НЕСЪЕДОБНО – *eh*ta nyesyed*ob*na – **This is inedible**
МОЖНО СЧЁТ, ПОЖАЛУИСТА? – *mozh*na shyot, pa*zhal*sta? – **May I have the bill, please?**
СДАЧИ НЕ НАДО – *sdach*i nye *na*da – **Keep the change**
НА ЧАЙ – na chai – **tip**

Restaurants, Bars and Cafés

*T*he choice of good eating and drinking establishments in both cities is rapidly expanding, though quality and price level see-saw dramatically. The following listings concentrate on the tried and trusted.

A few tips
An increasing number of restaurants accept credit cards, but it's wise to come well supplied with roubles. Very few now take foreign currency in cash even if the menu prices are quoted in dollars..

Vegetarians are poorly catered for in general. (If necessary, ask the waiter for help: *Ya nye yem myaso* – I don't eat meat; *Kakiye oo vas blyooda byez myasa?* – What dishes do you have without meat?)

Always book in advance (ask your hotel to do this). In winter, take a change of footwear to the restaurant rather than suffer wet boots all evening.

Tip as you would anywhere else in Europe (10 to 15 per cent). The cloakroom attendant will also expect a small gratuity.

Price guide
Poorer Russians seldom eat out and for the time being there is little sign of a middle class, so many restaurants are in the medium-to-expensive bracket. As a rough guide, reckon on the following categories per head without alcohol:

R less than $15 rouble equivalent
RR from $15 to $25
RRR $25 to $50
RRRR over $50

Beer costs between $3 and $8 per 500ml; vodka costs $3 to $7 per domestic bottle, twice that for imported. Wine and champagne vary considerably, locally-produced brands being greatly cheaper.

MOSCOW RESTAURANTS
RUSSIAN
Amsterdam RR
Pleasant, affordable Russian/Dutch joint venture with good Russian country food.
Pyatnitskaya Ulitsa 4 Building 30. Tel: 231 9725. Metro: Tretyakovskaya.

Boyarskiy Zal RRRR
Perhaps Russia's greatest restaurant. Russian 'baroque' cuisine, minstrels and stunning décor.
Metropol Hotel, Teatralniy Proezd 1/4. Tel: 927 6063. Metro: Teatralnaya Ploshchad.

Café Margarita R
Simple menu and live jazz attract artistic clientele. Picturesque setting.
Malaya Bronnaya Ulitsa 28. Tel: 299 6534. Metro: Mayakovskaya.

Glazur RRR
Carefully prepared Russian specialities. Diplomatic corps favourite.
Smolenskiy Bulvar 12. Tel: 248 4438. Metro: Smolenskaya.

Kropotkinskaya 36 RRR
One of the capital's first – and best – private restaurants. Romantic ambience.
Ulitsa Prechistenka 36. Tel: 201 7500. Metro: Kropotkinskaya.

Russkoe Bistro R
This growing chain of very inexpensive fast-food restaurants aims to combat the foreign burger invasion with tasty Russian favourites like *koulibiaca* (fish *en croûte*) served with *kvass* (black bread beer).
Tverskaya Ulitsa 19 and Bolshoy Gnezdnikovskiy Pereulok 10. Metro: Tverskaya.

Slavyanskiy Bazaar RR
Raucous Soviet-era restaurant with
Cossack dancers, acrobats ...
Nikolskaya Ulitsa 7. Tel: 921 1872. Metro:
Lubyanka.

Soyuz Pisatelyei (The Writers'
Union) RRR
Aristocratic cuisine and open fireplace in
ex-dining room of Soviet literati.
Ulitsa Vorovskovo 52. Tel: 291 2169.
Metro: Barrikadnaya.

Stanislavskovo 2 RRR
Small, exclusive and extremely well run.
Reservations essential.
Leontevskiy Pereulok 2. Tel: 291 8681.
Metro: Arbatskaya.

Syedmoye Nyebo (Seventh Heaven)
R/RR
Bad food but tremendous view from
revolving restaurant in TV tower.
Ulitsa Korolyova 15. Tel: 282 2293. Metro:
VDNKh. Phone for reservation and bring
passport and visa for security clearance.

U Babushki R/RR
'Granny's Place' excels with
unpretentious Russian home cooking.
Bolshaya Ordynka Ulitsa 42. Tel: 239
1484. Metro: Tretyakovskaya.

CAUCASIAN
Guria R
Cheap Georgian food,
lots of atmosphere, gypsy
band. Bring a bottle.
Komsomolskiy Prospekt 7.
Tel: 246 0378. Metro:
Park Kultury.

Iveria RRR
Spicy Caucasian
cooking, live music and
Stalin's favourite wines.
Ulitsa Rozhdestvenka 5/7.
Tel: 928 2672. Metro:
Lubyanka, Kuznetskiy
Most.

U Pirosmani RR
Georgian food served along with a
stunning view across the lake to
Novodevichiy Convent.
4 Novodevichiy Proezd. Tel: 247 1926.
Metro: Sportivnaya.

OTHER CUISINES
Les Champs Élysées RRR/RRRR
Fine French cooking and free limousine
pick-up service
Pullman Iris Hotel, Korovinskoe Shosse 10.
Tel: 488 8000.

McDonald's R
Bolshaya Bronnaya Ulitsa 29 (corner of
Pushinskaya Ploshchad). Metro:
Tverskaya, Pushkinskaya or
Chekhovskaya. Also at Ulitsa Arbat 50/52
(Metro: Smolenskaya) and Gazetniy
Pereulok 17/9 (Metro: Okhotniy Ryad).

Pizza Hut RR
Take-away and delivery services.
Kutuzovskiy Prospekt 17. Tel: 243 1727.
Metro: Kutuzovskaya. Also at Tverskaya
Ulitsa 12. Tel: 229 2013. Metro:
Tverskaya, Pushkinskaya or Chekhovskaya

Santa Fe RR/RRR
Big, friendly Mexican restaurant with
attentive staff, sensible prices and a
wonderful menu.
Mantulinskaya Ulitsa
5/1 Building 6. Tel: 256
1487. Metro: Ulitsa
1905 Goda.

TrenMos RR
US-run expatriate oasis
of pasta, burgers,
Miller beer and good
service
Komsomolskiy Prospekt
21. Tel: 245 1216.
Metro: Park Kultury.

The ubiquitous McDonald's
– Moscow boasts three

ST PETERSBURG RESTAURANTS

RUSSIAN

Café 01 R
Small and popular, good food and imported draught beer.
Karavannaya Ulitsa 5. No telephone – book in person. Metro: Gostiniy Dvor.

Imperial RRR
Elegant, *ancien régime* interior with good Russian specialities.
Kamenoostrovskiy Prospekt 53. Tel: 234 3296. Metro: Petrogradskaya.

Izmailov RRR
Fixed-rate dinner, folk entertainments.
6-ya Krasnoarmeiskaya Ulitsa 22. Tel: 292 6838. Metro: Baltiyskiy Vokzal.

Landskrona RRRR
Petersburg's best. Top-class dining and roof-top patio.
Nevskiy Palace Hotel, Nevskiy Prospekt 57. Tel: 275 2001. Metro: Mayakovskaya.

Literaturnoe Café RR/RRR
Pushkin's favourite (then Café Wulf et Béranger). Overrated but attractive.
Nevskiy Prospekt 18. Tel: 312 8536. Metro: Nevskiy Prospekt.

Sudarynya RR
Good-value food from medieval recipes.
Ulitsa Rubinshteina 28. Tel: 312 6380. Metro: Gostiniy Dvor.

Troyka RRR
Exuberantly decorated, good cabaret, reasonable Russian food.
Zagorodniy Prospekt 27. Tel: 113 5343. Metro: Vladimirskaya.

CAUCASIAN

Baghdad Café R
Down-to-earth eatery serving good-quality Azerbaijani dishes.
Furshtadskaya Ulitsa 35. Tel: 272 2355. Metro: Chernyshevskaya.

Pirosmani RR
Small-scale but well-thought-of restaurant decorated after the peculiar style of the eponymous Georgian artist.
Bolshoy Prospekt 14. Tel: 235 6456. Metro: Petrogradskaya then trolleybus.

Tbilisi R/RR
Reasonable Georgian outfit. Small but popular. Live music.
Sytninskaya Ulitsa 10. Tel: 232 7548. Metro: Gorkovskaya.

OTHER CUISINES

Daddy's Steak House RR
Steak, pasta and salad bar.
Moskovskiy Prospekt 73. Tel: 252 7744. Metro: Frunzenskaya.

The Europe Restaurant RRRR
Art nouveau décor and high quality French cuisine. Excellent Sunday jazz brunch.
Grand Hotel Europe, Mikhaylovskaya Ulitsa 1/7. Tel: 119 6000. Metro: Nevskiy Prospekt.

Senat-Bar RRR
Continental food, exotic interior and dozens of different imported beers.
Galernaya Ulitsa 3. Tel: 314 4920. Metro: Nevskiy Prospekt.

Tandoor R/RR
Fairly authentic Indian restaurant. Cheap, with pleasant staff.
Voznesenskiy Prospekt 2. Tel: 312 3886. Metro: Nevskiy Prospekt.

MOSCOW BARS AND CAFÉS

BARS

The Armadillo Bar
Tex-Mex saloon a stone's throw from Red Square. Darts, pool, country music and great guacamole.
Khrustalniy Pereulok 1. Tel: 298 5258. Metro: Ploshchad Revolyutsii.

BB King's
Posters of jazz and blues greats, appropriate live music, bar food.

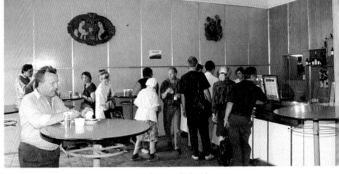

Moscow café providing quick snacks for people in a hurry

Sadovaya-Samotechnaya Ulitsa 4. Metro: Tsvetnoy Bulvar.

Rosie O'Grady's
Very convincing imitation of a pub with draught Guinness, Sky Sport and Sunday lunches.
Corner of Ulitsa Znamenka and Ulitsa Malaya Znamenskiy. Metro: Aleksandrovskiy Sad, Arbatskaya.

The Shamrock Bar
Lots of foreign students, businessmen and tourists supping Guinness.
Irish House, Ulitsa Novy Arbat 19. Metro: Arbatskaya.

The Sports Bar
Dozens of TV sets relay satellite sports broadcasts, plus pool, table soccer and dance floor.
Ulitsa Novy Arbat 10. Metro: Arbatskaya.

CAFÉS
Art Café Cappuccino
Italian coffee, draught beer and light eats in café that doubles as gallery.
Nikitskiy Bulvar 12. Metro: Arbatskaya.

Kombi's
Freshly-filled jumbo rolls, toasted sandwiches and milkshakes.
Sadovaya-Triumfalnaya Ulitsa 1. Metro: Mayakovskaya. Also at Prospekt Mira 46/48. Metro: Prospekt Mira.

Restaurant Bar Italia
Expensive attempt at continental summer café culture.
Ulitsa Arbat 46. Metro: Smolenskaya.

Sadko Arcade
Contains a cluster of relatively cheap western-style snack joints.
Krasnogvardeiskiy Proezd 1. Metro: Ulitsa 1905 Goda.

ST PETERSBURG BARS AND CAFÉS
BARS
The Bier Stube
Comfortable but pricey Tyrolean bar within the Nevskiy Palace hotel.
Nevskiy Prospekt 86. Metro: Mayakovskaya.

Chaika
German bar with wurst and sauerkraut.
Kanal Griboyedova Naberezhnaya 14. Metro: Nevskiy Prospekt.

John Bull Pub
Imitation British pub close to Moscow rail station on Nevskiy Prospekt.
Nevskiy Prospekt 79. Metro: Mayakovskaya.

Mollie's Irish Bar
Good pub food and welcoming atmosphere. The city's best bar.
Ulitsa Rubinshteina 36. Metro: Gostiniy Dvor.

CAFÉS
Café St Petersburg
Nice selection of good food. Crowded.
Kanal Griboyedova Naberezhnaya 3. Metro: Nevskiy Prospekt.

The Chameleon
Small café near the *Aurora* Cruiser. Good value hot dishes and Turkish coffee.
Ulitsa Kuybysheva 33/8. Metro: Gorkovskaya.

Le Café
Up-market light snacks, excellent coffee.
Nevskiy Prospekt 142. Metro: Ploshchad Vosstaniya.

VODKA

'**D**rinking is the joy of Russians,' declared Prince Vladimir in 988. A millennium later, Russians are still hard at it, consuming more alcohol than any other Europeans – on average nearly three times as much as the British.

The national drink is vodka, meaning 'little water', reputedly invented by Russian monks in the 14th century. Produced

from filtered water and pure spirit, it is drunk neat, chilled and in one gulp, traditionally followed by a bite of pickled cucumber or a deep sniff from a chunk of black bread – said to help it go down more smoothly.

The ingredients of the commercially manufactured article vary slightly: *Stolichnaya* includes a little sugar syrup, *Moskovskaya* has a drop or two of vinegar added and *Pshenichnaya* is made from distilled potatoes. Other brands are infused with lemon oil, peppers or bison grass.

By contrast, *samogon* – moonshine – is made from whatever comes to hand. Rye, wheat, sugar and potatoes are the ingredients of choice, but Russians are adept at creating homebrew from toothpaste, boot polish – even cockroach powder. Journalists reporting the war in Chechnya were plagued with Russian requests for colour photographic film, a key ingredient of an especially lethal infusion.

The choice of brands goes on and on ...Vodka is an essential aspect of Russian culture, its consumption prodigious by Western standards

Peter the Great's troops received two mugfuls daily by imperial decree. Peter established the state monopoly on vodka production, and used the proceeds to help finance his wars. Today, vodka revenues rake in more than income tax: one million bottles a day are sold in Moscow alone.

A secret report, commissioned by the government in 1980, concluded that drinking had become a threat to national security. It spurred Gorbachev to cut vodka production drastically in the hope of forcing the population back to the workplace. But the policy succeeded only in driving production underground and emptying shops of sugar, potatoes and eau de Cologne, while employees spent ever longer queueing for the few bottles that remained on sale – then drank their contents.

Hotels and Accommodation

*I*n the days when tourism was a state monopoly, the foreign traveller was lucky to know in which hotel he was to be housed before arrival at the airport. Happily, the situation has changed for the better. Although Russia's hotel industry still has some catching up to do, you can now enjoy first-class standards of accommodation – if you can afford it.

The adventurous might consider staying with a Russian family for an unrivalled insider's view of what life is really like.

The first step
Russia is slowly adjusting to normal tourist practices, but for the time being one rule makes for a considerably more enjoyable trip – choose and book accommodation with your travel agent before arrival. There are no equivalents of the booking agencies in the west which can allocate travellers at short notice to comfortable, middle-grade hotels – partly because there are no comfortable, middle-grade hotels.

Good-quality, western-style hotels are few and often heavily booked. Their ex-Soviet counterparts are frequently all but empty, yet the barrage of paperwork,

calls to the police and hostile reception staff that greet unexpected arrivals are a serious disincentive to fully independent travel. At the very least, book your St Petersburg accommodation while you are in Moscow (and vice versa).

(See page 175 for bed and breakfast booking.)

Selecting a hotel
Neither Moscow nor St Petersburg has the huge number of affordable hotels and guest houses that characterise, say, London or Paris. This simplifies your choice.

Western-run hotels are four or five star, mostly operated by chains such as Radisson or Marco Polo, and are all one would expect from an international luxury

The monolithic Rossia Hotel near Moscow's Red Square. It can accommodate 6,000 guests

The Ukraine Hotel in Moscow overlooks the Moskva river

hotel, the tariff included. Expect to pay between $200 and $300 for a double room.

Ex-Soviet establishments are notably cheaper (the better ones cost around $100 for a double, the less pleasant as little as $20), but are generally spartan, unloved and under-maintained. Their own star grading system is a deceptive guide to the quality within. Broken televisions, eccentric plumbing, drunken trade union delegations and vermin are not considered grounds for a discount. Four stars is the top of the range and the least likely to offer the above inconveniences. Take an experienced travel agent's advice.

COME PREPARED

If you are booked into a Soviet-style hotel, bring your own toilet paper and soap and a razor in case there is no shaver point. It is also worth being equipped with a universal bath plug since very few Russian hotel bathrooms sport this convenience. Contrary to popular opinion, this is not because plugs were overlooked in the communist command economy or that they were beyond the means of the country that put the first man in space. Simply, Russians prefer to wash in running water.

Location

Most western-style hotels are situated in the centre of both cities. Those which are not offer a regular shuttle service to and from the centre. Location is more critical with regard to Soviet-style hotels, many of which are in industrialised suburbs: the savings may not be worth the trouble of commuting into town each day. Check the location carefully before booking.

Having chosen the hotel, ask for a room that does not face the street. Russian traffic runs on low-grade petrol – the smell can be overpowering – and at night you run the risk of being kept awake by the noise.

Finding the way to your hotel may well be easier than understanding the procedure there

Understanding your hotel

There should be no difficulties with a western-style hotel. You will find most staff speak English. Restaurants, gymnasiums and souvenir shops are liberally distributed about the premises. Breakfast is usually included in the room price (you generally have the choice from an extensive buffet) and credit cards are accepted. Most will also offer facilities for changing money and many are equipped with state-of-the-art business centres.

Soviet-style establishments, however, work according to their own sub-culture, which takes some adjusting to.

With your key you will be issued a pass essential to getting past the doorman later. Always lock your door and do not open it to unknown visitors under any circumstances. The key should be left with the old lady manning your floor, the *dezhurnaya*, who can also serve you tea or at least hot water.

The hotel's restaurants and bars may keep illogical hours – it is worth

The lavish interior of the ground-floor restaurant in the Metropol Hotel, Moscow

checking to avoid disappointment later. Breakfast is rarely included in the room price and credit cards are almost never acceptable.

Checking out can be a time-consuming process since the *dezhurnaya* will want to inspect your rooms to ensure towels etc are all intact. Give yourself ample time if you have a plane or train to catch!

Hostels

A good option for the budget conscious is the traveller's hostel, aimed at western backpackers but clean and secure and an excellent source of camaraderie and local knowledge. Accommodation is generally in dormitories though some two-bed rooms are available. A communal breakfast is offered in the

Youth hostel in St Petersburg – a cheap and cheerful option if money is tight

sections for rental advertisements. Most flats are very basic by western standards of comfort. Those with modern electrical appliances and a fresh coat of paint are likely to be as expensive as rented accommodation in any other major capital. However, it works out much cheaper than a hotel.

For camping possibilities, see page 179.

Bed and breakfast
Living with a Russian family is the ideal way to get acquainted with life beyond the holiday brochures and tour buses. It is also surprisingly well organised in both cities and can be pre-booked prior to arrival.

Prices per night vary but range from around $20 to $30 for rooms checked by agency staff and for a mammoth Russian breakfast. Most of the hosts either speak fluent English or are students keen to improve their grasp of the language. Some may be happy to work as a driver for the duration of your stay or might offer their services as a guide to the city.

For Moscow, contact **Moscow Bed and Breakfast**, tel: (095) 192 2514, fax (095)152 7493. In the US, this organisation is connected to **Russian Travel Service**, PO Box 311, Fitzwilliam, NH 03447. Tel/fax: (603) 585 6534. It can also assist with arranging travel documents, theatre tickets, car rental, etc.

For St Petersburg, contact **Shakti Centre**, tel/fax: (812) 279 5198, who can also be reached through Russian Travel Service and offer similar additional assistance.

morning and self-catering facilities are available for general use.

There is one well-known hostel in each of the two cities and booking ahead of a planned trip is essential to avoid disappointment, especially during high points of the season such as the St Petersburg White Nights. Both are under foreign management and the staff speak English. They can also help arrange visa invitations (see page 178) and organise travel tickets within Russia between Moscow and St Petersburg or something as exotic as the Trans-Siberian Railway.

In St Petersburg, call (812) 277 569; in Moscow, call (095) 971 4059.

Self-catering
Self-catering accommodation in furnished apartments is not a feasible short-term option, but those planning to stay for a month or more should check the English-language press classified

On Business

*E*conomic reforms in the former Soviet Union have opened the floodgates of investment opportunities for foreign business. The rapidly developing market has given Moscow and St Petersburg a frontier atmosphere of enterprise, leading observers to refer ironically to the new 'Wild East'.

BUSINESS CENTRES

Most western-style hotels have business centres, and both cities can provide communications, translation/ interpretation and printing services.

Moscow:

Americom

Also offers office leasing.
Radisson Slavyanskaya Hotel, Berezhkovskaya Naberezhnaya 2. Tel: 941 8427.

Artel Business Centre
Ulitsa Novy Arbat 2, Tel: 291 3374.

Comstar Business Centre
Petrovskiy Passazh 3rd floor, Ulitsa Petrovka 10. Tel: 975 2319.

St Petersburg:
Grand Hotel Europe Business Centre
Mikhaylovskaya Ulitsa 1/7. Tel: 119 6000.

Neptun Business Centre
Obvodnovo Kanal Naberezhnaya 93a. Tel: 210 2707.

BUSINESS CLUBS

In Moscow:

Moscow Commercial Club
Bolshaya Kommuisticheskaya Ulitsa 2a. Tel: 274 0081.

In St Petersburg:

Association of Joint Ventures
Kazanskaya Ulitsa 36, room 602. Tel: 312 7954.

St Petersburg American Association
Tel: 273 0108.

BUSINESS TRAVEL

Hotel bookings, flight arrangements and transfers can be arranged through the **Thomas Cook** offices in Berlin:
Reisebüro Helios GmbH, Uland Strasse 73, 10717 Berlin, Germany. Tel: (49) 30 86 000527.

American Express Travel Services are based in Moscow at: *Sadovaya-Kudrinskaya Ulitsa 21a. Tel: 956 9000.* In St Petersburg: *Grand Hotel Europe, Mikhaylovskaya Ulitsa 1/7. Tel: 119 6009.*

For extra special meetings in Moscow you can hire limousines with drivers from:

Sunrise Limousines. *tel: 366 4656.*

Express Motors. *tel: 198 0034.*

The business centres in hotels such as this are a boon for foreign business people

Western-style hotels always have their own fleets of taxis, usually Mercedes.

COMMERCIAL SECTIONS

The commercial section of your embassy in Moscow may be able to help with current trading information and put you in touch with partners and colleagues.
UK: *Kutuzovskiy Prospekt 7/4.*
Tel: 956 6052-3.
US: *Novinskiy Bulvar 15.*
Tel: 252 2451-59.
Ireland: *Grokholskiy Pereulok 5.*
Tel: 280 6500.

COMMUNICATIONS

Better hotels offer satellite links for calls. Fax modems and many private telephones are now capable of good international communications. Some business centres can arrange temporary e-mail accounts. Another option for AT&T calling card holders is available in Moscow – to be connected on, call 155 5042 and quote your number. If you are not a card holder, you can still use the service to make collect calls to the US.

Finally, a series of satellite telephones in Moscow is operated by Comstar communications. Call 250 2131 for details of the closest. In St Petersburg, several international pay phones have been installed in the city centre. Instructions are provided in several different languages and credit cards are on sale widely.

CONFERENCE CENTRES AND EXHIBITION HALLS

Most western-style hotels offer conference facilities. Listed below are the main trade exhibition sites. For advice on putting on your own show, consult the business centres (see opposite) or contact the following institutions:

Moscow:
All-Russia Exhibition Centre
(VVTs/VDNKh)
Prospekt Mira. Tel: 181 6355.
Expocentre
Sokolnicheskiy Val 1a. Tel: 268 1340.
International Trade Centre Exhibition Complex
Krasnopresnenskaya Naberezhnaya 12. Tel: 256 6180.

St Petersburg:
LenEXPO Exhibition
Bolshoy Prospekt 103. Tel: 217 1112.
Perspective
Moskovskiy Prospekt 220a. Tel: 293 5497.

CONSULTANCY

Many major western accountants/consultants are already well established:
Arthur Andersen
Staraya Basmannaya Ulitsa 14, Moscow. Tel: 262 5077. Bolshoy Prospekt 10, St Petersburg. Tel: 350 4984.
Coopers and Lybrand
Ulitsa Schepkina 6, Moscow. Tel: 288 9801. Bolshaya Morskaya Ulitsa 39 (Astoria Hotel #528), St Petersburg. Tel: 210 5528.
Ernst and Young
Podsosenskiy Pereulok 20/12, Moscow. Tel: 297 3322. Ulitsa Gogolya 11, St Petersburg. Tel: 312 9918.
Price Waterhouse
Bolshoy Strochenovskiy Pereulok 22/25, Moscow. Tel: 230 6185.

GRAPHICS AND PRINTING

Printing, photocopying and design services are offered in Moscow by **AlphaGraphics**, *Pervaya Tverskaya Yamskaya Ulitsa 22 (tel: 251 1215)* and in St Petersburg by **Kella Design and Printing**, *Kronverskaya Ulitsa 10 (tel: 232 1890).*

Practical Guide

CONTENTS

ARRIVING
Visas and registration

All visitors to Russia need a visa. Package tourists can rely on the tour operator to deal with the bureaucrats. If you are travelling independently, apply for a visa to the Russian embassy in your own country or, to avoid officialdom and rudeness, have a specialist agency arrange your visa (see below).

The Business Visa, valid for up to two months, is the simplest type to obtain even if you have no intention of engaging in trade during your stay. Visa agencies can provide the necessary invitation from a Russian company. No invitation is required for a Tourist Visa, but you must show proof of pre-paid accommodation for each night of the proposed trip. A Visitor Visa requires a personal invitation from a Russian.

You must register your visa with UVIR (department of visas and registration) within 24 hours of arrival. Hotels deal with this for their guests but visitors in private accommodation should see to it themselves – without registration you will have difficulty extending your stay.

UVIR's office in Moscow is at Ulitsa Pokrova 42 (*metro: Kurskaya, Krasnie Vorota*), tel: 207 0239. In St Petersburg, the chief UVIR department is at Saltykova-Shchedrina Ulitsa 4 (*metro: Nevskiy Prospekt*), tel: 278 2481.

For a visa extension, approach your hotel or tour operator first – UVIR office rank among the most frustrating places on earth.

The following travel agencies abroad specialise in Russia and can arrange visas

Alpha-Omega Travel, Amadeus House, 6 Lidgett Lane, Garforth, Leeds, LS25 1EQ, UK. Tel: 0113 2862121.

BMT Inc, 19 West Street, 34th Floor, New York, NY10004, USA. Tel: 212 422 0091.

The Russia House, 37 Kingly Cour Kingly Street, London W1R 5LE, UK. Tel: 0171 439 1271.

Finland Station, one of St
Petersburg's rail termini

Time Travel,
42 Southwark Street,
London SE1 1UN,
UK. Tel: 0171
357 0308.

By air
Moscow's airport is
Sheremetevo II. To
obtain up-to-date
information on international flights, you
should call 156 8019.

The airport is a half-hour drive from
the city and the best (but most
expensive) means of getting to the centre
is by taxi. Taxis are actually just privately
owned cars whose drivers throng the
arrival hall in the hope of picking up a
fare. Be prepared to bargain hard, but
even so you should usually expect to pay
about $40–50. A far cheaper, but slower
and more complicated option, is to take a
bus (from the terminal beyond the car
parks). No 551 goes to Rechnoy Vokzal
metro station and no 517 to Planernaya
metro station – both of which are on the
outskirts of town.

St Petersburg's international airport is
Pulkovo II. For current information on
international flights, call 104 3444.

The airport is situated 17km south of
the city. Taxis are a slightly cheaper
means of travelling in St Petersburg than
in Moscow and the bus no 13 route runs
close to the city centre, stopping at
Moskovskaya Ploshchad.

By rail
Those arriving in Moscow by train from
western Europe come into Belorusskiy
Vokzal (Station), served by the metro's
circle and green lines. Trains to St

Petersburg from Helsinki pull into
Finlandskiy Vokzal at Ploshchad Lenina
metro, while those from London and
Berlin arrive at Varshavskiy Vokzal, close
to Baltiyskaya metro.

CAMPING
Moscow has two motels-cum-campsites.
Neither is close to the centre of town and
both are insecure.
Mozhayskiy, Mozhayskoe Shosse 165.
Tel: 446 2335. Open: June to mid-
September.
Butovo, Butovo. Tel: 381 7734. Open:
June to mid-September.

Of St Petersburg's two options
(below), the first is preferable.
Retur, Primorskoe Shosse km 29.
Tel: 237 7533.
Olgino, Primorskoe Shosse km 18.
Tel: 238 3550.

CHILDREN
Children up to seven travel free on public
transport. Aeroflot allows one child
under five to travel with each
accompanying adult on its internal
flights. Most museums and parks offer
discount tickets for children. Disposable
nappies and baby foods are on sale in
most western-style supermarkets (see
page 143).

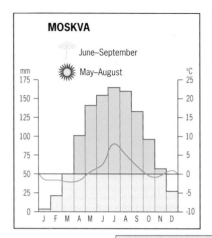

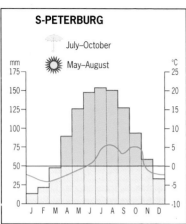

CLIMATE

St Petersburg is slightly warmer than Moscow, but the damp and the Baltic breezes can make it seem colder. March and early April bring slush and puddles during the thaw. Mid-May to mid-September sees temperatures averaging 18°C in both cities, often reaching 25–30°C in July and August. Winter draws in quickly by mid-October.

CONVERSION TABLES

See tables opposite.

CRIME

The tourist is unlikely to encounter the much-reported organised criminal activity. Petty theft is comparable to that in major cities elsewhere. Don't leave valuables unattended, don't carry large amounts of cash, and always lock your hotel room. Be wary if a stranger invites you home. At night, be careful with taxi rides and keep to well-lit streets. Avoid the gangs of gypsy children in areas frequented by foreigners – they strip their victims of valuables like locusts. On overnight trains lock your compartment door and don't open it to strangers – there are reports of travellers being gassed and robbed in their sleep.

WEATHER CONVERSION CHART

25.4mm = 1 inch

$°F = 1.8 \times °C + 32$

CUSTOMS

Russian customs regulations are many and ever changing, but real problems only arise if you try to export tradable quantities of commodities like caviar, or antiques. This means steering clear of genuine icons and *objets d'art* (including books) produced more than 20 years ago. Items of military hardware and uniforms are also best avoided. Permits to export antiques and art *are* available through the Ministry of the Environment in Moscow (tel: 254 8072) or the Ministry of Culture (tel: 248 0903).

Fill in a currency declaration form on arrival, get receipts for each time you change money and fill in a similar form on departure. Roubles may not be exported.

DRIVING

Russian driving practices are hair-raising, and travelling by car in Moscow and St Petersburg is not recommended. Roads are pot-holed and badly signposted, and you are at the mercy of the GAI, the ill-reputed traffic police.

Drivers must possess an international driving licence. Russians often drive without insurance, so have a comprehensive policy (if driving a rented car, check the level and conditions of cover). It is illegal to drive after drinking any amount of alcohol.

Traffic drives on the right. The speed limit in built-up areas is 60kph, 90kph in unpopulated areas and 120kph on highways. Petrol – *benzin* – comes in several octane grades, 95 being the best for western cars. Unleaded is non-existent.

Car hire agencies operating in Moscow and St Petersburg include:
Avis: Moscow, tel: 578 5646. St Petersburg, tel: 312 63 18.
Europcar: Moscow, tel: 253 1369.
Hertz: Moscow, tel: 578 7532. St Petersburg, tel: 277 4032.

ELECTRICITY

Most of Russia runs on 220v and uses continental European-style 2-pin plugs. Many electrical stores and western supermarkets sell adaptors.

EMBASSIES AND CONSULATES
Moscow (embassies):
Australia: Kropotkinskiy Pereulok 13. Tel: 956 6070.
Canada: Starokonyushenniy Pereulok 1. Tel: 241 5882.
Republic of Ireland: Grokholskiy Pereulok 5. Tel: 288 4101.
New Zealand: Ulitsa Vorovskovo 44. Tel: 290 3485.

Conversion Table

FROM	TO	MULTIPLY BY
Inches	Centimetres	2.54
Feet	Metres	0.3048
Yards	Metres	0.9144
Miles	Kilometres	1.6090
Acres	Hectares	0.4047
Gallons	Litres	4.5460
Ounces	Grams	28.35
Pounds	Grams	453.6
Pounds	Kilograms	0.4536
Tons	Tonnes	1.0160

To convert back, for example from centimetres to inches, divide by the number in the third column.

Men's Suits

UK	36	38	40	42	44	46	48
Rest of Europe	46	48	50	52	54	56	58
US	36	38	40	42	44	46	48

Dress Sizes

UK	8	10	12	14	16	18
France	36	38	40	42	44	46
Italy	38	40	42	44	46	48
Rest of Europe	34	36	38	40	42	44
US	6	8	10	12	14	16

Men's Shirts

UK	14	14.5	15	15.5	16	16.5	17
Rest of Europe	36	37	38 39/40	41		42	43
US	14	14.5	15	15.5	16	16.5	17

Men's Shoes

UK	7	7.5	8.5		9.5	10.5	11
Rest of Europe	41		42	43	44	45	46
US	8	8.5	9.5	10.5	11.5	12	

Women's Shoes

UK	4.5	5	5.5	6		6.5	7
Rest of Europe	38	38	39	39		40	41
US	6	6.5	7	7.5		8	8.5

UK: Sofiyskaya Naberezhnaya 14. Tel: 230 6333.
USA: Novinskiy Bulvar 19/23. Tel: 252 2451-9.
St Petersburg (consulates):
UK: Proletarskoy Diktatury Ploshchad 5. Tel: 312 0072.
USA: Furshtadskaya Ulitsa 15. Tel: 274 8235.

EMERGENCY TELEPHONE NUMBERS

The following can be called free of charge in both cities from any public telephone:
Fire 01
Police 02
Ambulance 03
Gas 04
   In the event of theft or illness, a better bet is to turn to your hotel or embassy.

HEALTH

Your travel insurance policy should give good cover for medical treatment. Russian hospitals are grim, foreign-staffed clinics expensive. Both cities offer well-stocked pharmacies, but travellers are advised to bring their own prescribed medications and contraceptives. No injections are mandatory before arrival, though some doctors advise diphtheria and hepatitus inoculations. AIDS is present of course.

   Moscow's tap water is allegedly safe, St Petersburg's is not. Stick to bottled water where possible.

   In an emergency, either speak to your embassy doctor or contact the following medical clinics or pharmacies:

Clinics
American Medical Centre, Shmitovskiy Proezd 3, Moscow. Tel: 956 3366.
European Medical Centre, Gruzinskiy Pereulok 3, Moscow. Tel: 253 0703.
American Medical Centre, Reki Fontanki Naberezhnaya 77, St Petersburg. Tel: 119 6101.

Pharmacies
Sana, Ulitsa Nizhnaya Pervomaiskaya 65, Moscow. Tel: 464 1254.
Litpharm, Ulitsa Chernyakovskaya 4, Moscow. Tel: 155 7080.
Vita, Ulitsa Poklonnaya 6, Moscow. Tel: 249 7818.
Damian, Moskovskiy Prospekt 22, St Petersburg. Tel: 110 1744.
Pharmadom, Nevskiy Prospekt 5, St Petersburg. Tel: 312 7078.
   Before travelling, up-to-date advice on health matters is available from Thomas Cook travel consultants.

LANGUAGE

Pronunciation

With a few exceptions, Russian words are pronounced the way they are read. Knowing which syllable to stress, however, takes experience. Just speak slowly and hope for the best.

А/а – ah in 'bar'

Б/б – b

В/в – v

Г/г – g except in words like *Грозного* when it is pronouced as a v

Д/д – d

Е/е – yeh in 'yes'

Ё/ё – yoh in 'yoghurt'

Ж/ж – zh in 'treasure'

З/з – z

И/и – ee in 'Eden'

Й/й – softer than the above, like the y in 'joy'

К/к – k

Л/л – l

М/м – m

Н/н – n

О/о – oh in 'fort' when stressed, otherwise ah in 'bar'

П/п – p

Р/р – r, rolled like an Italian r

С/с – s

Т/т – t

У/у – oo in 'school'

Ф/ф – f

Х/х – kh in the Scottish 'loch'

Ц/ц – ts in 'pretzel'

Ч/ч – ch in 'church'

Ш/ш – sh in 'shoe'

Щ/щ – shch in 'fresh cheese'

Ы/ы – i in 'ilk' but more guttural

Э/э – e in 'end'

Ю/ю – yoo in '*u*niverse'

Я/я – ya in 'yard'

Ь, Ъ – soft sign and hard sign – both affect preceding consonant

Basic words and phrases

yes – da – *ДА*

no – nyet – *НЕТ*

please – pa*zh*a*l*sta – *ПОЖАЛУИСТА*

thank you – spas*ee*ba – *СПАСИБО*

excuse me/I'm sorry – izvin*ee*tyeh – *ИЗВИНИТЕ*

good morning – *do*broye *oo*tra – *ДОБРОЕ УТРО*

good afternoon – *do*bry dyen – *ДОБРЫЙ ДЕНЬ*

good evening – *do*bry *vyech*er – *ДОБРЫИ ВЕЧЕР*

good night – spako*i*ny *no*chi – *СПОКОЙНОЙ НОЧИ*

I have... – oo men*ya*... – *У МЕНЯ...*

I haven't... – oo men*ya* nyet... – *У МЕНЯ НЕТ...*

Do you speak English? – Vwi gavar*ee*tyeh pa angl*ee*sky? – *ВЫ ГОВОРИТЕ ПО АНГЛИЙСКИЙ?*

I do not understand – Yah nye pani*mah*yoo – *Я НЕ ПОНИМАЮ*

Repeat it, please – Pavtar*ee*tyeh pa*zh*a*l*sta – *ПОВТОРИТЕ ПОЖАЛУИСТА*

May I?/Do you mind? – *Mozh*na? – *МОЖНО?*]

How much does... cost? – *Sko*lka *stoy*it... ? – *СКОЛЬКО СТОИТ...?*

when – kag*dah* – *КОГДА*

yesterday – vche*rah* – *ВЧЕРА*

today – se*vod*nyah – *СЕГОДНЯ*

tomorrow – *za*vtra – *ЗАВТРА*

at what time..? – vah *sko*lka ..? – *ВО СКОЛЬКО...?*

where is..? – gdyeh..? – *ГДЕ...?*

here – zdyes – *ЗДЕСЬ*

there – tam – *ТАМ*

near – bl*ee*zka – *БЛИЗКО*

far – dale*koh* – *ДАЛЕКО*

behind – zah – *ЗА*

opposite – na *pro*tiv – *НАПРОТИВ*

in front of – py*ered* – *ПЕРЕД*
to the right – na *prava* – *НА ПРАВО*
to the left – na *lye*va – *НА ЛЕВО*
straight on – vper*yod* – *ВПЕРЁД*
street – *oo*litsa – *УЛИЦА*
petrol station – benzaka*lon*ka – *БЕНЗОКОЛОНКА*
airport – ayero*port* – *АЭРОПОРТ*
railway station – vok*zal* – *ВОКЗАЛ*
platform – plat*for*ma – *ПЛАТФОРМА*
bus stop – asta*nov*ka – *ОСТАНОВКА*
metro station – *stahn*tsia me*troh* – *СТАНЦИЯ МЕТРО*
price – tse*na* – *ЦЕНА*
ticket office – *kas*sa – *КАССА*
ticket – bil*yet* – *БИЛЕТ*

Quantity
one – a*deen* – *ОДИН*
two – dva – *ДВА*
three – tree – *ТРИ*
four – chet*eeri* – *ЧЕТЫРЕ*
five – pyat – *ПЯТЬ*
six – shyest – *ШЕСТЬ*
seven – syem – *СЕМЬ*
eight – *voh*syem – *ВОСЕМЬ*
nine – *dye*vyat – *ДЕВЯТЬ*
10 – *dye*syat – *ДЕСЯТЬ*
100 – stoh – *СТО*
1,000 – *tee*syacha – *ТИСЯЧА*
a little – nyem*noh*ga – *НЕМНОГО*
enough – *khvah*tit – *ХВАТИТ*
many/much – *mnoh*ga – *МНОГО*
too many/too much – *sleesh*kom *mnoh*ga – *СЛИШКОМ МНОГО*

Days and months
Monday – pani*dyel*nik – *ПОНЕДЕЛЬНИК*
Tuesday – *vtor*nik – *ВТОРНИК*
Wednesday – sry*edah* – *СРЕДА*
Thursday – chet*vyehrg* – *ЧЕТВЕРГ*
Friday – *pyat*nitsa – *ПЯТНИЦА*
Saturday – soo*boh*ta – *СУББОТА*
Sunday – voskres*enyeh* – *ВОСКРЕСЕНЬЕ*
January – yan*var* – *ЯНВАРЬ*
February -fev*ral* – *ФЕВРАЛЬ*
March – mart – *МАРТ*
April – ap*ryel* – *АПРЕЛЬ*
May – mai – *МАЙ*
June – i*yoon* – *ИЮНЬ*
July – i*yool* – *ИЮЛЬ*
August – *ahv*goost – *АВГУСТ*
September – sent*yahbr* – *СЕНТЯБРЬ*
October – akt*yabr* – *ОКТЯБРЬ*
November – na*yabr* – *НОЯБРЬ*
December – de*kabr* – *ДЕКАБРЬ*]

Foreign papers are sometimes sold on kiosks

MAPS AND ADDITIONAL INFORMATION

The best maps of Moscow and St Petersburg are printed by Russian Information Services (28 East State Street, Montpelier, VT 05602 USA. Tel: 802 223 4955). They are included in the directories *Where in Moscow* and *Where in St Petersburg*, both widely available in Russia.

The *Traveller's Yellow Pages*, published for both cities by InfoServices International Inc (1 Saint Mark's Place, Cold Spring Harbor, NY 11724 USA. Tel: 516 549 0064), contain a wealth of practical information in English; obtainable in hotel lobby kiosks.

MEDIA

Foreign newspapers are on sale in hotels and western supermarkets. Several local English-language newspapers are available free, of which *The Moscow Times* is best. The entertainments listings are invaluable.

Most hotels are well-equipped with CNN and satellite broadcasts. The Moscow local TV channel shows BBC news in English at 7.45am weekdays and 7.00am at weekends.

BBC radio's World Service broadcasts on 1260kHz medium wave.

MONEY MATTERS

One rouble is theoretically divided into 100 kopecks but in practice the lowest denomination in circulation is the one rouble coin.

Don't change money on the streets since both city centres are littered with bureaux de change – *obmyen valyuty* – and private deals remain illegal. Since inflation erodes the rouble rate daily, change small amounts at a time. Banknotes printed before 1993 are no longer legal tender. Dollars and Deutschemarks are the easiest to change, but torn or marked bills, old-style Deutschemarks and pre-1988 dollars are often refused. Travellers' cheques are widely accepted: bring US dollar denomination cheques in small values.

In case of theft, Thomas Cook MasterCard cheques can be refunded by reporting the loss on (44) 1733 318 950 (reverse charges).

Credit cards are generally only accepted in foreign-run shops, hotels, larger restaurants and travel agents. Some banks offer cash advances on Visa and MasterCard. In case of theft, phone Moscow (095) 284 4784 or 284 4151. American Express is based in Moscow at Sadovaya-Kudrinskaya Ulitsa 21A (tel: 956 9004) and in St Petersburg in the Grand Hotel Europe, Ulitsa Mikhaylovskaya 1/7 (tel: 315 6517).

OPENING HOURS

Shops open Monday to Saturday 9am–6 or 7pm. Larger stores stay open until 8pm and many of them, including foreign-run supermarkets, trade on Sundays. Many kiosks, especially around railway stations, are open 24 hours a day.

PHOTOGRAPHY

Military bases and the like remain off limits, and militia officers may object if you point a lens directly at them (if so, take note). Otherwise you are unlikely to encounter problems.

Film, including Polaroid cartridges, is widely available, but any video cassettes other than VHS format should be brought from home. Express developing and printing points are easy to find in both cities. Try **Servistsentr** in Moscow (Ulitsa Novy Arbat 17) or **Agfa** in St Petersburg (Nevskiy Prospekt 20).

PLACES OF WORSHIP
Moscow:
Catholic Chaplaincy: Karmanitskiy Pereulok 6. Tel: 243 9621.
Protestant Chaplaincy: Ulitsa Olaf Palme 5 korpus 2. Tel: 143 3562.
Synagogue: Arkhipova Ulitsa 14. Tel: 923 9697.
Mosque: Vypolzov Pereulok 7. Tel: 281 3866.
St Petersburg:
Roman Catholic Church of Our Lady Of Lourdes: Kovenskiy Pereulok 7. Tel: 272 5002.
Synagogue: Aleksandrovskoy Fermy Proezd 2. Tel: 264 3981.
Mosque of the Congregation of Muslims: Kronverkskiy Prospekt 7. Tel: 233 9819.

POST
Stamps, postcards and envelopes can be bought in most hotels, but the Russian postal service is best not relied upon for important letters and packages.

The following international courier agencies operate out of both cities:
DHL Tel: 956 1000 (Moscow); 311 2649 (St Petersburg).
TNT Tel: 156 5893 (Moscow); 273 6007 (St Petersburg).
Federal Express Tel: 253 1641 (Moscow); 279 1287 (St Petersburg).
UPS Tel: 430 6373 (Moscow); 312 2915 (St Petersburg).

PUBLIC TRANSPORT
Metro
The metro systems are cheap, clean, efficient and safe even at night. A grasp of the Cyrillic alphabet is essential to making sense of the signs.

A neon letter M (red in Moscow, blue in St Petersburg) indicates a station entrance. *ВХОД* (*Vkhod*) on the swing doors means entrance, *ВЫХОД* (*Vykhod*) exit. Tokens (*zhetoni*) are on sale at the *kassa* (cash desk), but a modest outlay will buy a monthly season ticket (on sale till the 8th of each month) either for the metro alone (*Proezdnoy*) or overground transport as well (*yedeeni bilyet*). Signs overhead and on the walls indicate which platform to wait at.

On the train, you are expected to give up your seat to old people and women with children. On arrival, a recorded voice announces the station and the connections to other lines. To get out, head for the *ВЫХОД В ГОРОД* (*vykhod v gorod*) sign. If there is more than one exit, the sign indicates which takes you where. To change lines, look for *ПЕРЕХОД* (*perekhod*) – meaning crossing – to adjoining stations, indicated by a figure walking up steps on a blue background.

The metro in both cities opens before 6am and last changes must be made by 1am in Moscow and 11.30pm in St Petersburg. The metro map for Moscow is on pages 26–7 and for St Petersburg on pages 24–5.

Buses, trams and trolleybuses
To make full use of the overground networks requires a high degree of insider knowledge. Tickets valid for all three are sold in strips of 10 and can be bought from the drivers. You punch them yourself in the contraptions inside the vehicle. See also pages 26–7.

Suburban trains
Many sights outside the city are best reached by the suburban trains, known as *elektrichka*. Tickets, bought at the railway station from the *prigorodny kassi* (often located in a separate part of the station), are very cheap. On the platform, the train will be identified by its final

T-shirts frequently carry ironic messages referring back to the days of communist rule

destination which you should check on the diagram in the ticket hall. Not every train stops at each station, so check with fellow passengers before boarding.

Taxis

Stopping a cab (*taksi*) is simple, especially in the centre of town – hold your arm out and a queue of eager drivers will soon pull up. Official cabs (marked by a 'T' in a circle) are equipped with meters, but raging inflation has made them obsolete. The fare should be agreed before you get in (bear in mind that fares are rapidly approaching world levels). If necessary, write down the fare and the destination.

Many 'taxis' are simply private cars or government vehicles whose drivers are earning a little on the side. They are cheaper, but a degree of caution is advisable. Never get in a car which already has passengers and do not let the driver pick up additional fares on the way. Women travelling alone at night should avoid taxis completely.

Taxis can be booked from your hotel or by telephone: in Moscow, call 927 0000 or 457 9005; in St Petersburg, call 312 0022, 356 9329 or 298 3648. Allow

at least an hour. Many western-run hotels have their own cabs which are far superior to the local service but much pricier.

Travelling between Moscow and St Petersburg

The easiest and cheapest method is by overnight train, leaving either city around midnight and arriving around 8 or 9am. The 'Intourist' and 'Krasnaya Strela' services are the most comfortable. Many hotels will arrange your journey for you, but independent travellers should come with passport to the station to buy a ticket in advance. In Moscow, Leningradskiy Vokzal (Leningrad Station) is at Komsomolskaya Ploshchad 3 (metro: Komsomolskaya), tel: 266 9111. In St Petersburg, Moskovskiy Vokzal (Moscow Station) is at Nevskiy Prospekt 85 (metro: Ploshchad Vosstaniya), tel: 168 4597.

Alternatively, use the central ticket offices at Malaya Kharitonevskiy Pereulok 6 (metro: Chistie Prudiy), tel: 262 0604 in Moscow, or Yekaterinskiy Kanal Naberezhnaya 24 (metro: Nevskiy Prospekt), tel: 162 3344 in St Petersburg.

NB: See **Crime** (page 180) for special precautions.

TELEPHONES

Public phones in Moscow operate either on brown plastic tokens (*zhetoni*) sold in metro stations, or one rouble coins.

St Petersburg has new international call boxes which operate on cards sold in hotels, kiosks and larger shops. Instructions are available in foreign languages. Ordinary phones and the metro system run on the same metal tokens, sold in the stations. Pick up a few at the beginning of your trip in case of emergencies and keep a note of your hotel telephone number.

For an intercity call on local lines, dial 8 and wait for the tone. The code for Moscow is 095, for St Petersburg 812. The country code for Russia is 7.

To call internationally, dial 8, wait for the tone, and dial 10 before the country code.

Faxes and telegrams can be sent from international telegraph offices in Moscow at Tverskaya Ulitsa 7, and in St Petersburg at Bolshaya Morskaya Ulitsa 3/5.

See also **On Business** page 176.

TIME

Both cities run three hours ahead of GMT, eight hours ahead of New York time. Summer time, when clocks go forward an hour, begins on the last Saturday of March and ends on the last Saturday of October.

TIPPING

With the exception of taxi drivers, who invariably charge double for foreigners, tip as you would anywhere else in the world.

TOILETS

Russian public toilets are rare and dreadful. Go out armed with paper and make use of restaurant or museum facilities, which are marginally better.

The hammer and sickle remain as architectural details on a Moscow building

Suitably god-like, the statue in Moscow of Yuri Gagarin, first man in space

Kommunisticheskaya Ulitsa 3/9 Building
1. Tel: 271 2609.
Gryphon Travel, Hotel Ukraine room
743. Tel: 243 2595.
Story-M Travel, Novokonyushenniy
Pereulok 9 korpus 2. Tel: 244 7260.
SVO Travel, Ulitsa Novy Arbat 15 room
1820. Tel: 202 2293.
Time Travel, Ulitsa Pistsovaya 12.
Tel: 257 9220.
St Petersburg:
Gryphon Travel, Moskva Hotel,
Aleksandra Nevskovo Ploshchad 2.
Tel: 274 0022.

TOURIST INFORMATION
There are no tourist information offices
in either city. Hotel service bureaux are
the best source of advice.

TOURS IN THE CITIES
A good way to get your bearings is to
take a city tour. Moscow's best group,
'Patriarshiy Dom' (tel: 255 4515), runs
guided tours in English, including a
purpose-built Moscow orientation trip
and walking tours. In St Petersburg, the
'Shakti' centre (tel: 279 5198) organises
a wide range of tours, including 'In the
Days of Peter the Great,' 'Russian
Literature' and an 'Art Collector's Tour'.

TRAVEL AGENCIES
A number of companies take telephone
bookings for internal and international
flights. Some arrange hotel reservations
and car hire.
Moscow:
Addams and Ruffle, Ulitsa Kosygina
19. Tel: 939 0200.
Barry Martin Travel, Malaya

TRAVELLERS WITH DISABILITIES
Russia offers little to ease a disabled
person's trip. Access to the metro and
other forms of public transport is all but
ruled out and few buildings other than
better-class hotels have wheelchair ramps.
However, Russians often go out of their
way to lend a hand in a tricky moment.
   The London-based organisation
Mobility International (tel: 0171 403
5688) may be able to assist with more
detailed enquiries.

WOMEN TRAVELLERS
Most western-type supermarkets and
pharmacies stock tampons and sanitary
towels.
   The attitude to women of some
Russian men may seem chauvinistic but is
not intended to offend. However, if you
feel sexually harassed, cause a public
scene rather than ignore it. At night, keep
off back streets and avoid lone taxi rides.
'Mace' spray canisters are legal in Russia.
   In Moscow, the **Women's Crisis
Centre** (tel: 244 3449) runs a hotline for
foreigners which can help in an emergency.

ACKNOWLEDGEMENTS
The Automobile Association wishes to thank the following photographers, libraries and associations for their assistance in the preparation of this book.
THE BRIDGEMAN ART LIBRARY 34/5, 61a
MARY EVANS PICTURE LIBRARY 12, 12/13, 13, 35, 60, 61c, 112a, 113a, 113b
REX FEATURES LTD 14, 15, 17a, 17b, 87
RUSSIA & REPUBLICS PHOTOLIBRARY 127a, 131, 152/3, 154
SPECTRUM COLOUR LIBRARY 86/7
TRIP 84 (N J Wiseman), 85 (I Kolpakova), 127b (A Tjagny-Rjadno), 134 (V Kolpakov), 135a (B Konov), 135b (N Chesnokov), 155 (V Sidoropolev), 159 V Kolpakov)
ZEFA PICTURES Cover, 152, 153
All remaining pictures are held in the Associaiton's own library (AA PHOTO LIBRARY) with contributions from J N ARNOLD 8/9, 26, 28, 32, 33, 36, 39, 40a, 40b, 41a, 48, 50, 53a, 57, 58, 63, 65, 79, 88, 92/3, 94, 99, 105, 106, 107, 108, 109, 110, 112b, 128, 137, 140, 141, 142, 144b, 145a, 145b, 149b, 151, 161, 162, 163, 171b, 171c, 174b, 175, 184; K PATERSON 1, 2, 4, 5, 6, 10, 16, 18, 19, 20a, 20b, 21, 22, 23, 29, 30, 37, 38, 41b, 42/3, 44, 46a, 46b, 49, 51a, 51b, 52a, 52b, 53b, 55, 56, 59, 61b, 62, 71, 73, 75, 77, 80, 81, 82, 83, 86, 90, 91, 92, 93, 95, 96/7, 98, 100, 101, 102, 103, 104/5a, 104/5b, 114, 115, 117, 119, 125, 129, 130a, 130b, 132, 133, 136, 138, 139, 143, 144a, 147, 149a, 157a, 157b, 158, 167, 169, 170a, 170b, 171a, 172, 173, 174a, 176, 178, 182, 187, 188, 189

CONTRIBUTORS

Series adviser: Melissa Shales **Project editor:** Nia Williams **Designer:** Design 23 **Copy editor:** Audrey Horne **Verifiers:** Christopher and Melanie Rice **Indexer:** Marie Lorimer **Proof-reader:** Sheila Hawkins